10.

KdV

STRAND PRICE
$5 00
7/2023

D0856456

High Victorian Design

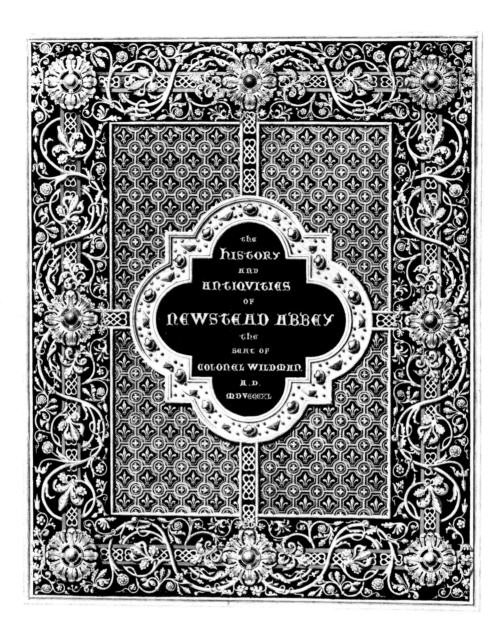

Design for a title page for *The History and Antiquities of Newstead Abbey, the Seat of Colonel Wildman, A.D. MDVCCXL*, by Henry Shaw (1800–1873). Thomas Wildman (1787–1859) had purchased Newstead Abbey from Lord Byron in 1817, with a fortune fleeced by his father from the millionaire collector, William Beckford (1760–1844). This 1840 title, never published, prefigures the antiquarian, Gothic, naturalistic and geometrical aspects of High Victorian design.

HIGH VICTORIAN DESIGN

SIMON JERVIS

The Boydell Press

© Simon Jervis 1983

First published 1983 by

The Boydell Press
an imprint of Boydell & Brewer Ltd
PO Box 9, Woodbridge, Suffolk IP12 3DF

ISBN 0 85115 187 6

Produced by Bettina Tayleur Ltd
1 Newburgh Street, London W1V 1LH

Designed by Grant Gibson
Typeset in Ehrhardt by Rowland Phototypesetting Ltd,
Bury St Edmunds, Suffolk
Printed in Singapore by Imago Publishing Ltd,
Thame, Oxfordshire

Cover/jacket/title page
The typeface used on the cover, jacket and title page comes from *A Glossary of Ecclesiastical Ornament* (1844), by A. W. N. Pugin (1812–52). This is one of four alphabets in Pugin's *Glossary*; the original has the letters alternately in blue and red. The *Glossary* comprises ecclesiastical designs by Pugin and a learned text quoting from such authorities as Durandus (1237–96). The *Ecclesiologist* called for imitation.

Contents

(1724–30) is an unusually early example of an antiquarian approach: more usually at this stage Gothic was a mode contrasted with Palladian, as by William Kent at Rousham, Oxfordshire (1738–41), or used for picturesque effect, as by Sir John Vanbrugh at Blackheath, London (1717). In the Rococo period interior Gothic became widespread, often combined or associated with Chinese decoration, and Batty Langley, the major promoter of Gothic, systematized it into a series of quasi-classical orders in his *Ancient Architecture Restored* (1742), an achievement which earned him the undying contempt of Victorian Gothicists.

The foundation in 1717 of the Society of Antiquaries of London provided a focus for the study of national antiquities. In 1744 the antiquary, William Stukeley, who was closely involved in the foundation of the Society, designed a bridge at Boughton, Northamptonshire, which, although prompted by archaeology, presented a very Rococo appearance. A reverse progression took place at Horace Walpole's Strawberry Hill, Twickenham, which began in 1749 as a Rococo folly directed by a highly conventional Palladian, William Robinson, and ended as a monument of the picturesque owing much to James Essex, a serious student of Gothic. It incorporated a multitude of details copied from Gothic monuments – often, it must be admitted, with little regard to scale or congruity.

Walpole was one of many wealthy dilettanti who encouraged interest in Gothic – notably John Chute, Sanderson Miller, and Sir Roger Newdigate: their houses, the Vyne, Hampshire, Radway Grange, Warwickshire, and Arbury Hall, Warwickshire, are among the *incunabula* of the Gothic Revival proper. The archaeological approach of the Neo-classicist, exemplified by Stuart and Revett's *Antiquities of Athens* (1762), was paralleled by deeper researches into Gothic, such as Captain Francis Grose's *Antiquities of England and Wales* (1783–7), John Carter's *Specimens of Ancient Sculpture and Painting* (1786), Richard Gough's *Sepulchral Monuments of Great Britain* (1786), and William Halfpenny's *York* (1795).

But Gothic was in practice more often a picturesque, or even sublime, contrast to Grecian than an exercise in archaeology. The masterpiece of sublimity was Fonthill Abbey, Wiltshire (1796–1807) designed by James Wyatt for William Beckford. Picturesque productions range from Robert Adam's neat, castellated castles to John Nash's own house, East Cowes Castle, Isle of Wight, Hampshire (c. 1798) and Sir Jeffry Wyatville's remodelling of Windsor Castle, Berkshire (1824–40).

The success of Gothic was due not only to architects and antiquaries. Gothic novels from Horace Walpole's *The Castle of Otranto* (1765) to C. R. Maturin's *Melmoth, the Wanderer* (1820) and Sir Walter Scott's Waverley Novels (1814–32), an unparalleled series of bestsellers by an author of genius, as well as poetry by Scott himself, Thomas Chatterton's *Rowley Poems* (1777) and John Keat's *Eve of St Agnes* – all this established the mediaeval period as a proper interest for every person of taste, instead of a barbarous and deservedly neglected dark age.

14

And not only interest was aroused but also sympathy, a sympathy which inspired both that chivalric farce the Eglinton Tournament (1839) and the passionate interest in Gothic of John Ruskin, a fervent reader of Scott.

In the first third of the nineteenth century Gothic was satisfactorily, if not finally, analysed. Thomas Rickman's *An Attempt to Discriminate the Styles of English Architecture* (1817) gave a clear, logical and chronological account of the progress of Gothic, and many editions, with continuous enlargement and improvement, are a witness to Rickman's success as both archaeologist and propagandist. A. C. Pugin and E. J. Wilson's *Specimens of Gothic Architecture* (1821–3) provided illustrations of a clarity and accuracy which equalled Rickman's writings. Pugin and Wilson were sponsored by John Britton, the most influential architectural publisher of the early nineteenth century, a self-made man who published an endless stream of works on antiquarian matters from 1800 until his death in 1856, including the fifteen volumes of *The Cathedral Antiquities of Great Britain* (1814–35).

Private collectors played an important part in the dissemination of antiquarian knowledge. Already in the late eighteenth century Samuel Hieronymus Grimm had been employed as an antiquarian topographer by Sir Richard Kaye, Dean of Lincoln Cathedral, and Sir William Burrell. Turner was used in this capacity by Walter Fawkes of Farnley Hall, Yorkshire, among many others, and John Buckler by Thomas Lister Parker of Browsholme Hall, Yorkshire, also one of many. At Charlecote, Warwickshire, George Hammond and Mary Elizabeth Lucy created from 1826 onwards an Elizabethan Revival ensemble with advice from Thomas Willement, stained glass designer, heraldic expert, and decorator. At Goodrich Court, Herefordshire, Sir Samuel Rush Meyrick employed Edward Blore, whose book *Monumental Remains* (1826) was an important source for designers, to create a Gothic setting for his collections, including a 'Hastilude Chamber' for his celebrated armour. Meyrick was closely associated with Henry Shaw, whose *Specimens of Ancient Furniture* (1836) and *Decorative Arts of the Middle Ages* (1851) set a high standard of both scholarship and chromolithography.

In the domestic context Tudor and Elizabethan architecture and decoration were as successful as Gothic proper, and the terms of the competition for the New Palace of Westminster in London (the Houses of Parliament) specified a Gothic or Elizabethan design. Thomas Hunt's *Tudor Architecture* (1830) and C. J. Richardson's *Architectural Remains of the Reigns of Elizabeth and James I* (1840) are among the pioneering studies, but Joseph Nash's *The Mansions of England in the Olden Times* (1839–49), with its superb atmospheric lithographs, established the beau ideal of the Elizabethan country house. Hardwick Hall, Derbyshire, one of the houses illustrated by Nash, was refurbished at this date, and in 1843 Lord Lytton began to 'restore ' his ancestral home, Knebworth, Hertfordshire, in a mixture of Gothic and Elizabethan. J. C. Loudon, prolific writer on architecture, gardening, and farming, was an advocate of the Elizabethan style for the country house, and Wollaton, Nottinghamshire, which contained late-sixteenth-century Gothic Revival elements, was imitated by Sir Charles Barry at Highclere in about 1840, and by Lewis Vulliamy at Westonbirt, Gloucestershire, in about 1850.

The incorporation of early fragments is rare in architecture (Highcliffe, Hampshire, which incorporates part of a house from Les Andelys in Normandy, is an example), but in the 1830s it was a commonplace of interior decoration. Already in 1826 the auctioneering firm of Christie's had held a sale of carving for this purpose; A. W. N. Pugin decorated rooms at Scarisbrick, Lancashire, with a pot-pourri of Flemish carvings; Loudon reports on the trade in carvings, and there is evidence that fake old Flemish carvings were manufactured in large quantities in Malines, Belgium, for export to England.

Antique dealers, cabinet-makers, and designers combined to cater for this taste. Among the dealers with antiquarian knowledge were George Bullock (associated with Scott's work at Abbotsford, his home in Roxburghshire), John Webb, John Swaby, Daniel Terry, Edward Baldock, and Samuel Pratt; their names crop up again and again in connection with the major decorative schemes executed in early- to mid-nineteenth-century England. A significant development is that it became not uncommon for a house to be furnished almost entirely with antiques. A noteworthy example is Pryor'sbank, London, a Gothic house built by the antiquary and collector Thomas Baylis in the late 1830s and filled by him with old carvings, furniture, armour, paintings, ceramics, and sculpture, ranging from Gothic to Italian Baroque. Cotehele, the Cornish seat of the Mount Egcumbe family since the fifteenth century, was refurbished at about the same date and with a similar effect.

Designers and professional antiquaries occupied an intermediate status between private patrons and dealers. Willement was an adviser for Charlecote; Richard Bridgens, whose *Furniture and Candelabra* (1838) contained interesting Elizabethan designs, worked with George Bullock at Abbotsford, and also designed furniture for Aston Hall, Birmingham. J. R. Planché, like Willement, was an heraldic expert, and C. J. Richardson was architect, antiquary, designer, and draughtsman.

A consequence of the fashion for decoration in earlier styles was the emergence of craftsmen capable of producing imitations of Gothic and Renaissance ornament. Two contrasting examples are Thomas Jordan who invented a pioneering wood-carving machine, which could rough out Gothic tracery automatically (hand-finishing was still required), and W. G. Rogers, a virtuoso woodcarver who could imitate Gothic, Italian Renaissance, or Grinling Gibbons carving of the late-seventeenth century with remarkable accuracy. (His son, W. H. Rogers, was an equally versatile designer.)

The revival of encaustic tiles by Mintons at Stoke-on-Trent, Staffordshire, and other firms at Worcester, Worcestershire, and Ironbridge, Shropshire, is a similar case of supply meeting demand. This particular demand was stimulated by the discovery of a remarkable series of mediaeval tiles in the Chapter House at Westminster; among those involved was Lewis Nockalls Cottingham, important as an architect and designer and the publisher of a series of full-size illustrations of mediaeval carvings, and also as a collector of architectural fragments on a grand scale.

Another collection was assembled during the rebuilding of the Palace of Westminster, London, to provide examplars for the carvers working on its decoration. Although the competition for the New Palace had been won by Sir Charles Barry and he exercised full control over its design, virtually all of its decorations were in the hands of A. W. N. Pugin, the creative antiquary *par excellence.*

Pugin's father, A. C. Pugin, was an antiquary and topographer as well as a designer in a competent Regency Gothic mode. The young A. W. N. Pugin worked for his father as a draughtsman and did some Regency Gothic designs which he later deplored. But by the mid 1830s he had developed a much deeper insight into and sympathy for the working of Gothic architecture and ornament. His books were passionate propaganda for Gothic as the only proper Christian style, and a number of rich patrons, including Charles Scarisbrick and Lord Shrewsbury, allowed him to put his ideals into practice. But the decoration of the New Palace of Westminster was his crowning achievement, and he drove himself to death working out designs for furniture, ceilings, carpets, tiles, metalwork, heraldry – every detail of every interior in that vast building. It is Pugin's remarkable gift that, although he never combines or invents motifs in a way which he believed unjustified by precedent, the result is not a dry reconstruction but interiors full of colour, movement, and life.

Pugin was without a peer as a designer of ornament, but there were other architects whose capacity to re-create in the language of earlier styles was equal to his. Anthony Salvin is an example: at Harlaxton, Lincolnshire (begun 1831), Mamhead, Devon (1828), and Peckforton, Cheshire, (1846–50) he worked with great conviction in the High Elizabethan, Tudor, and Castellated styles. Although they often made of it something rather more formally original than Pugin or Salvin had done, the Reformed Gothic of the High Victorian Goths was also founded on a deep knowledge of earlier precedent, a knowledge which is particularly evident when they were engaged in the restoration of earlier buildings.

George Edmund Street's *Brick and Marble in the Middle Ages* (1855), R. Norman Shaw's *Architectural Sketches from the Continent* (1858), W. E. Nesfield's *Specimens of Mediaeval Architecture* (1862), and William Burges's *Architectural Drawings* (1870) are evidence of a new development: the increasing importance of Continental precedents in the mid nineteenth century. (Admittedly Pugin had published many northern French examples earlier, but these were usually very similar to surviving English buildings known to him.) There was close contact with the leading Continental antiquaries, Adolphe-Napoléon Didron of the *Annales*

Archaeologiques (1844–72), August Reichensperger of the *Kölner Domblatt* (1842 –92), and Eugène Viollet-le-Duc, the greatest architectural historian and theorist of the age.

William Burges was the most antiquarian of the great Gothicists of the mid century. He was an avid collector of precious and curious objects, and designed for himself and his patrons objects in an antiquarian taste every bit as precious and curious. His restoration of Caerphilly Castle, for his great patron, the Marquis of Bute, was sensitive and scholarly, while Castle Coch (1875–81), also built for Bute, was a castle re-created, where the borderline between archaeology and originality is triumphantly blurred. Many of the restorations by George Edmund Street similarly transcend distinctions between copyism and creation, and Benjamin Bucknall's Woodchester Park, Gloucestershire (c. 1855–70), influenced by Viollet-le-Duc, demonstrated that even a comparatively unknown architect, adhering with conviction to Gothic precedent, could achieve originality.

A short essay such as this can only give an indication of the pervasive influence of antiquarian studies on design in the nineteenth century. But the role of the antiquary, the collector, and indeed the publisher in enriching the visual vocabulary of the designer and architect cannot be exaggerated. The study of earlier styles was not, as it might be now, a hobby for the creative artist; it was one of the main inspirations for his creation, and a discipline which informed his working methods. Of course, many Victorian designers, without the talents of a Pugin or a Burges, never went beyond copyism, and some even travestied the spirit of the originals. Yet it is right that these lesser talents be represented among the illustrations: they too are part of the period and only against their achievements can those of Pugin and Burges be measured.

2
Table from Mamhead, Devonshire, a house designed in the Tudor style by Anthony Salvin (1799–1881) from 1827 to 1833. A pair of similar oak tables, dating from 1838, are in the dining-room at Charlecote Park, Warwickshire, where Thomas Willement (1786–1871), best known as a stained glass designer, was responsible for the main decorative schemes. Willement also worked at Mamhead. The table is close to a design in Richard Bridgens, *Furniture with Candelabra and Interior Decoration* (1838). It exemplifies the early Elizabethen revival predilection for strapwork, bosses and pendants.

3

Standing cup and cover supplied to the Worshipful Company of Goldsmiths by Rundell, Bridge & Co., the Royal goldsmiths, in 1839 or 1840. This silver-gilt cup is directly based on a cup, dated 1554, presented to the Goldsmiths' Company by Sir Martin Bowes in 1561. The rock-crystal drum of the 1554 cup has been replaced by niches with mediaevalizing figures of Saints George, Andrew, Patrick and the Black Prince. The Goldsmiths' Hall, where the cup would have been displayed, was rebuilt to the designs of Philip Hardwick (1792–1870) in 1829 to 1835, incorporating Rococo Revival furniture within its Neo-classical façade.

4

Candlestick designed in 1844 to 1845 by A. W. N. Pugin (1812–52) for his own use in his new house, The Grange, Ramsgate. This gilt brass candlestick was made by John Hardman (1811–67) who had set up his own firm in 1838 and was by 1839 producing a complete range of church metalwork in the Gothic style to Pugin's design. Similar candlesticks were shown by Pugin at the Great Exhibition of 1851.

13

Highclere, Hampshire, remodelled by Sir Charles Barry (1795–1860) from 1838 to 1844 for the third Earl of Carnarvon (1800–49). Barry transformed a bleak classical house into a picturesque Elizabethan mansion enlivened with turrets, cresting and a great central tower. The formula is derived from Wollaton House, near Nottingham, designed by Robert Smythson in about 1580. Wollaton was also the model for Mentmore, Buckinghamshire (1850–5).

14
The Architectural Museum, Canon Row, Westminster, in about 1855. The Museum was founded in 1852; it included plaster casts and fragments of architecture from the collections of the architects Lewis Nockalls Cottingham (1787–1847) and Sir George Gilbert Scott (1811–78), the writer John Ruskin (1819–1900) and the Commissioners of Woods and Forests, who had collected examples of Gothic carving to inspire the craftsmen working on the New Palace of Westminster.

15
The Victoria Tower of the New Palace of Westminster in about 1860. The Victoria Tower, 336 feet high, stood above the royal entrance to the Palace, the greatest Gothic building of the age, designed by Sir Charles Barry (1795–1860), assisted on ornament by A. W. N. Pugin (1812–52). The buildings in the foreground which contrast so piquantly with the looming Gothic tower, were swept away to form Victoria Tower Gardens soon after this photograph was taken.

I

II

I   The Creative Antiquary

Frontispiece to *A Glossary of Ecclesiastical Ornament* (1844) by A. W. N. Pugin (1812–52). The *Glossary*, of which a second edition appeared in 1846, was one of the most distinguished early specimens of chromolithography. Its learned text was mainly by the Reverend Bernard Smith (1815–1903), an Anglican who in 1841 invited Pugin to superintend the painting of the chancel roof of his church, St Swithin, Leadenham, Lincolnshire, and who was received in 1842 into the Roman Catholic church at St Mary's, Oscott, Birmingham, where Pugin was 'Architect and Professor of Ecclesiastical Antiquities'.

II   The Creative Antiquary

Decanter, glass, silver, malachite, amethysts, crystal, jade and other semi-precious stones, designed by William Burges (1827–81), made by Richard Green, London, 1865. The design was first conceived in 1858: three such decanters were executed in 1865, two for Burges himself, and this example for James Nicholson. All three decanters, incorporating precious and exotic fragments such as Greek coins, Chinese jade, and Persian seals, evoke the treasures of St Denis as described in Abbot Suger's *De Administratione* of the late 1140s: many of these incorporated relics of pagan antiquity.

18

Cream jug, silver, by Benjamin Smith junior, London, 1841 to 1842. Benjamin Smith's father had worked for Rundell, Bridge and Rundell; he established an independent workshop in Camberwell in 1814. Benjamin Smith junior married a daughter of the pioneer of electroplating, G. R. Elkington (1800–65), and was involved in the Summerly's Art Manufactures design reform venture organized by Henry Cole (1808–82). This jug is freely adapted from a mid-eighteenth-century English prototype but its vigorous Rococo scroll and shell ornament is characteristically Victorian.

23

Framed panel of porcelain by Copeland & Garrett, about 1847. The picturesque landscape depicts Cochem on the Moselle; its border is boldly Rococo. Alderman William Taylor Copeland (1797–1868) was one of the great mercantile figures of the age, Lord Mayor of London in 1835. His partner from 1833 to 1847, Thomas Garrett, had been principal traveller to the Copeland firm. This panel belonged to the Museum of Practical Geology, founded in 1835 as an outgrowth of the Geological Survey, thanks to the energies of the Survey's director, Sir Henry De La Beche (1796–1855).

24

Framed panel of porcelain by Copeland, about 1847. This panel, which belonged to the Museum of Practical Geology, was probably intended to flank a fireplace. Its combination of floral painting and Rococo scrolls is typical. In 1844 Copeland & Garrett had registered a 'Louis Quatorze' border, with scrolls supporting floral swags. The art director of the firm, Thomas Battam (1810–64), encouraged the use of 'Etruscan' shapes and patterns, which he showed at the London 1851 Exhibition. He is unlikely to have approved of Copeland's Rococo productions, however marketable.

25

Binding of *Chit Chat or Short Tales in Short Words* (1850). The publishers of *Chit Chat*, Grant and Griffith, later Griffith and Farran, were successors to John Newbery (1713–67) the pioneer of children's books. This binding, green cloth blind-stamped and embossed in gold, may be compared with that used on *Fisher's Drawing Room Scrap Book* in 1844 and again in 1851. The author of *Chit Chat* (first edition 1825), Marie Elizabeth Budden, who died in 1832 aged 51, wrote sixteen books including *Valdimar; or the Career of Falsehood, Always Happy, A Key to Knowledge,* and *Claudine, A Swiss Tale.*

26

Design for drawing room upholstery and furniture, by Gillows of Lancaster, about 1830. This is one of many surviving designs by Gillows which illustrate the breakdown of eighteenth-century architectonic conventions of formality and symmetry in room arrangement. The variety of forms shown here is echoed by a wide range of style from stolid classicism in bookcase and side-table to florid scrolls in sofa and curtains. The use of rich acanthus ornament which had earlier preceded the development of the Rococo proper in the eighteenth century here heralds the Rococo Revival.

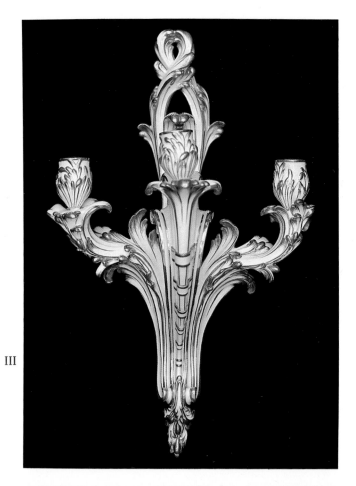

III

IV

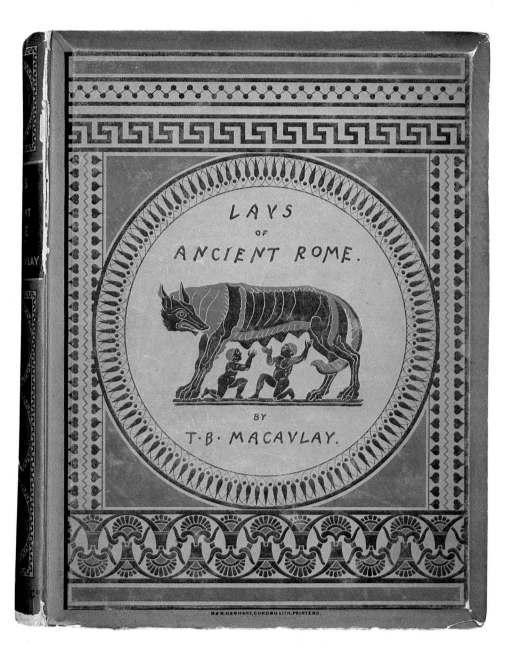

LAYS
OF
ANCIENT ROME.

BY

T·B· MACAVLAY.

M & N. HANHART, CHROMO LITH, PRINTERS.

V

III   The Rococo Revival
Girandole, porcelain, by Minton & Co. of Stoke-on-Trent, about 1853. This girandole was purchased by the Museum of Ornamental Art (now Victoria & Albert Museum) for £4 4s in 1853. This girandole is based upon a Sèvres model, the 'bras de cheminée Duplessis', which was in production from 1760 to 1765: Madame de Pompadour bought a pair in 1761. The particular specimen copied by Mintons was probably one owned by the banker Charles Mills (1792–1872).

IV   The Rococo Revival
A scene from *Le Bourgeois Gentilhomme*, by Charles Robert Leslie (1794–1859), 1841. Leslie showed further scenes from Molière plays, *Le Malade Imaginaire* and *Les Femmes Savantes*, at the Royal Academy in 1843 and 1845 respectively. The prominent gilt gesso table was supplied to Hampton Court Palace by James Moore in about 1715. Leslie doubtless intended it as Louis XIV in style, but, as with many Rococo Revival designers, precise archaeological accuracy eluded him.

V   Victorian Neo-Classicism
Binding of Thomas Macaulay, *Lays of Ancient Rome* (1847), designed by George Scharf (1820–95). This chromolithographed binding was 'in imitation of the ancient vases found in Italy at Vulci'. The Vulci excavations were commenced in 1828 by Lucien Bonaparte, Prince of Canino (1775–1846). Scharf, who also designed the scholarly illustrations to this 1847 edition of *Lays*, first published in 1842, was later involved in the design of the Greek, Roman and Pompeian courts at the Crystal Palace, Sydenham, opened in 1854.

27

Design for a chandelier with Sinumbra lamps, manufactured by Perry & Co., about 1830. Perry & Co. were founded in 1756 and enjoyed royal patronage under George IV, William IV and Queen Victoria. They were eventually taken over in 1925. This chandelier is in a rich classical acanthus style but its elaborate S-scrolls are on the border of Rococo, demonstrating how the Rococo Revival reflected general taste, and was not an isolated historicist episode.

28
Design for a canopy bedstead, by Thomas Charlton & Co., about 1865. In 1854 Charlton, Allen & Co. began to trade as cabinet-makers at 128 Mount Street, near Grosvenor Square. In 1861 the title of the firm changed to Thomas Charlton & Co.; it ceased trading in 1885. Mount Street was the best address in London for Victorian cabinet-makers: the leading firm of Holland & Sons moved there in 1852. This bed is a relatively refined example of High Victorian Rococo Revival.

impresario, Andrew Ducraux (Ducrow), in Kensal Green Cemetery, London; or in the pylons of Isambard Brunel's suspension bridge in Clifton, Gloucestershire, designed in 1829 but only completed in 1864; or in the goldsmith Stephen Smith's jug (1873) inspired by Egyptian examples illustrated in periodicals such as the *Art Journal*. The discovery of the remains of the Assyrian civilization by Sir Austen Henry Layard, described in his *Nineveh and Its Remains* (1848-9) and *Nineveh and Babylon* (1853), produced a minor and quasi-neo-classical Assyrian style, especially in ceramics and metalwork, around 1860.

At the London International Exhibition of 1862, along with such survivals of archaeological Neo-classicism as the firm of Sir James Duke & Nephews' Etruscan vases, and Pompeian-style objects of the 1860s, such as Howard & Sons' ebonized library furniture designed by Vandale, and J. M. Levien's Pompeian cabinet, there are the first glimmerings of that Neo-neo-classicism, the Adam and Louis XVI revival. Wertheimer of New Bond Street showed a console table 'after the renowned Gouthière' (the most celebrated French worker in ormolu of the late eighteenth century), and Wright & Mansfield of London showed furniture decorated with Wedgwood medallions in which 'the details of the whole are gleaned from the works of the Messrs (Adelphi) Adam and may be considered as indicating the style of English decorative furniture of the eighteenth-century'. At the Paris Exhibition of 1867 Wright & Mansfield's great Adam cabinet, later acquired by the South Kensington Museum, was one of the star pieces.

High Victorian Neo-classicism received little of the passionate loyalty accorded to Gothic; only Alexander Thomson set Grecian against Gothic, and vilified the latter. But Thomson was a comparatively obscure Glasgow architect. Gothic had John Ruskin on its side, and even the leading architects and critics who did not subscribe to Gothic, Professor T. L. Donaldson, James Fergusson, and Gottfried Semper, supported not Grecian, but an eclectic style based on the Renaissance. It is clear that the coldness, and lack of ornament or colour indelibly identified with Grecian were antipathetic to High Victorian taste. Although efforts were made to introduce ornament, movement, and polychromy, Neo-classicism was in decline during the High Victorian period. But, in Scotland and northern England, it continued to be the vehicle for masterpieces, and it cannot be overlooked in any account of High Victorian design which pretends to be comprehensive.

32

Cabinet, by Holland & Sons, about 1870. The general form of this cabinet and its gilt bronze mounts are directly based on French Neo-classical examples of about 1780. The refined marquetry includes directly classical elements in the engraved ivory panels with female figures derived from Thomas Hope, *Costume of the Ancients* (1809). A smaller version of the cabinet, supplied by Holland & Sons to R. N. Thornton in 1868, has refined naturalistic marquetry.

33

Pencil box, electrotype, made by Elkington, Mason & Co. of Birmingham in about 1854. The box was purchased by the Museum of Ornamental Art (now Victoria & Albert Museum) for £2 0s 6d in 1854. George Richards Elkington (1800–65) was, with his cousin Henry, the pioneer of electroplating; Josiah Mason, his partner from 1842 to 1859, was a wealthy pen manufacturer. The relief on the top of the box, depicting the story of Niobe, is based on ancient marbles now in Leningrad. The box was probably designed by Benjamin Schlick (1796–1872), a Danish architect employed by Elkingtons from about 1844.

34

Hand bell, bronze damascened with architectural ornaments in silver gilt and with a circle of female figures in silver, the handle of cornelian and silver gilt, by Barkentin & Slater, about 1864. This bell was purchased by the South Kensington Museum (now Victoria & Albert Museum) for £10 10s in 1864. Barkentin & Slater set up business as 'sculptors, silver, gold, & bronze manufacturers & workers in damascened steel' in 1864; in 1865 they had an appointment to the Princess of Wales. In 1868, however, Jes Barkentin, later of Barkentin & Krall, took over the business on his own as a goldsmith.

35
Jug, silver-gilt, designed and made by Stephen Smith, London, 1873. Stephen Smith was the grandson of one of the silversmiths who had worked for the celebrated firm of Rundell, Bridge and Rundell. This jug postdates his merger with A. B. Savory & Sons, who traded as The Goldsmiths' Alliance Ltd. It is based on an Egyptian prototype. Similar jugs were illustrated in the *Art Journal* (1847) and other periodicals, evidence of a continuing but intermittent interest in Egyptian design.

36

Jug, Parian ware, by Minton & Co. of Stoke-on-Trent, the design registered on 5 June 1852. This jug was purchased by the Museum of Manufactures (now Victoria & Albert Museum) for 2s in 1852. Its fluted Neo-classical refinement is in marked contrast to a similar Minton jug with bold fluting acquired by the Sèvres Museum in 1830. Mintons, who produced a prodigious variety of jugs, first marketed their Parian ware in 1847.

37
Bowl and stand, porcelain, by Kerr, Binns & Co. of Worcester, about 1854. This bowl and stand
were purchased by the Museum of Ornamental Art (now Victoria & Albert Museum) in 1854 for
15s 6d. A revival of late-eighteenth-century Neo-classicism was then in vogue; in 1854 the *Art
Journal* illustrated copies 'made at Coalbrookdale and shown by Messrs Daniell of Bond Street of
Neo-classical Sèvres vases in the Royal collection exhibited at Marlborough House in 1853'.

38

Bust of Clytie, Parian ware, manufactured by W. T. Copeland for the Art Union of London in 1855. Parian porcelain was first marketed in about 1845 by Copeland & Garrett, who became in 1847 W. T. Copeland. This bust was reduced from a well-known Greco-Roman marble in the British Museum by C. Delpech, who in 1861 reduced the head of the Apollo Belvedere for the Art Union of London. Clytie was singled out for praise in the *Art Journal* review of an exhibition of Parian ware held in Copeland's Bond Street premises in 1859. In 1867 the American sculptor Hiram Powers (1805–73) produced his own version of Clytie.

39

Figure of Beatrice, Parian ware, manufactured by W. T. Copeland in 1875, but published in 1864. The original marble, from which this porcelain figure is reduced, was by Edgar George Papworth junior, the son of a sculptor of the same name and the grandson of another, E. H. Baily (1788–1867); Papworth showed at the Royal Academy from 1852 to 1882. This figure, Gothic in subject and Neo-classical in style, illustrates the *Art Journal*'s praise of Parian ware in 1859 as 'delicate and refined in the highest degree' and 'eminently sculpturesque'.

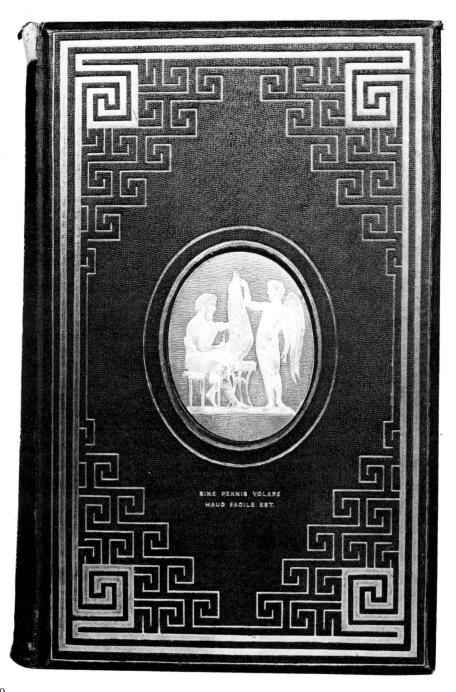

SINE PENNIS VOLARE
HAUD FACILE EST.

40

Binding of *Daedalus* (1860) by Edward Falkener (1814–96), brown cloth embossed in gold and white. Falkener, a widely travelled architect who excavated at Pompeii in 1847 and won a gold medal at the Paris 1855 Exhibition for his drawings of restorations, almost certainly designed this binding which was executed by Hanbury & Co. *Daedalus*, subtitled *The Causes and Principles of the Excellence of Greek Sculpture*, was dedicated to the Prussian and Bavarian people and included in an appendix a vigorous rebuttal of Ruskin's strictures on Greek art.

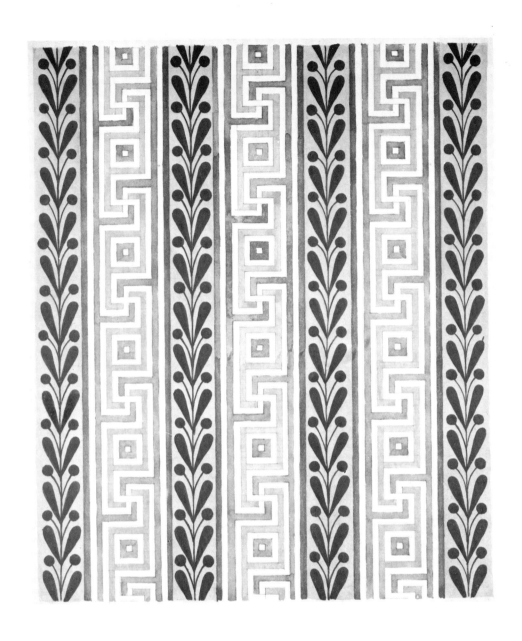

41
Wallpaper design by Owen Jones (1809–74), about 1860. This design, probably for Jackson &
Graham, combines a Greek fret taken from Plate XV of Jones's *Grammar of Ornament* (1856) with
a Greek laurel border from Plate XVII. The combination of the primary colours, yellow, red and
blue, with black and white reflects Jones's teaching on colour, strongly influenced by the French
colour theorist, M. E. Chevreul (1786–1889).

42
Carpet design by Owen Jones (1809–74) for Fishmongers' Hall, London, about 1865. Fishmongers' Hall is a Greek revival building of 1832 to 1835 designed by Henry Roberts (1803–76). Jones claimed that it had allowed him to realize his conception of Greek art, by introducing colour. His scheme was executed in 1865. Thomas Kershaw did the painting and gilding, Jackson & Graham supplied other decorative elements, and the carpets were by Templetons of Glasgow.

43
Monkwearmouth Railway Station, Durham, designed by John Dobson (1787–1865). The station belonged to the York, Newcastle and Berwick Railway and was considered a monument to its chairman, the 'railway king' George Hudson (1800–71), Member of Parliament for Sunderland from 1845 to 1859. Dobson had an immense architectural practice in the North of England, and, although he became a competent Goth, he continued to find clients for his dignified and correct classicism into the 1850s.

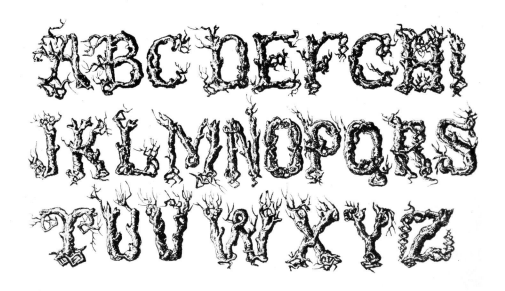

46
Rustic alphabet from F. Delamotte, *Examples of Modern Alphabets* (1859). Freeman Gage
Delamotte, the son of a painter, published many books on illumination and alphabets. *Modern Alphabets*, first published in 1858, achieved an eighteenth edition in 1935. This twiggy script may
be compared to the lettering designed by Richard Doyle (1824–83), for the title of *The King of the Golden River* by John Ruskin, first published in 1851 but written in 1841.

4

Naturalism

'Nature I loved; and next to Nature, Art': love of nature was one of the most universal and respected sentiments in the nineteenth century, and both John Ruskin and Christopher Dresser, otherwise an ill-assorted couple, would probably have agreed with Walter Landor's philosopher in his poem *Finis*. Naturalism, the use of nature as the basis of ornament, was both ubiquitous and various, and a reflection of a wider sympathy with nature, which prompted, for example, Luke Howard and Thomas Forster's meteorological studies, John Constable's paintings, the geological works of Sir Charles Lyell and William Smith, the crazes for ferns and shells, and ultimately, Charles Darwin's *Origin of Species* (1859).

Romantic feelings about nature, as expressed in poetry by William Wordsworth or John Clare, were slow to have any effect on the repertoire of ornament. An early symptom was the work of George Bullock, who, in the few years before his death in 1818, pioneered the use of native plants for inlaid decoration on his furniture, which was executed in native woods. Richard Brown's *Rudiments of Drawing Cabinet and Upholstery Furniture* (1920) contained a panegyric of Bullock, who did much work for Sir Walter Scott at Abbotsford, Roxburghshire, where he co-operated on the interior decoration with Scott's architect, William Atkinson. Atkinson also worked for the wealthy banker and collector Thomas Hope, at his house, The Deepdene, Surrey. The taste which began in about 1820 for dense acanthus ornament, which later merged into the scrolls of the Rococo Revival, had a naturalistic aspect, particularly in silver, where pieces formed entirely of organic scrolls begin to appear in the 1830s. Rococo silver in the eighteenth century had used natural forms for ornament and these reappeared in, for example, Frederick Knight's *Vases and Ornaments* (1833). Similar pieces, basically Rococo in form, but encrusted with ever more naturalistic flowers and fruit, continued to be made into the 1850s. The use of suitable plants for the basic shape of utensils was a development introduced from France in the 1840s; in 1851, for instance, Winfields of Birmingham, the brass-bed manufacturers, showed curtain-hooks in the form of fuchsias and anemones. 'The Mimosa or Flower Cornet by W. B. Pine' (1851) may also be mentioned; it was, according to the *Journal of Design*, 'an elegant arrangement of flowers in the form of a wreath, and intended to be worn by ladies . . . who are suffering from deafness. The principal flower in the wreath forms an ear-trumpet.' Plants were also used for the cast relief decoration of

basically simple earthenware jugs manufactured in the Staffordshire Potteries from the early 1840s onwards, and metalwork was also often overlaid with a layer of leafage.

The use of naturalistically sculpted plants for ornament was an encouragement to the revival of woodcarving, led by W. G. Rogers, a versatile carver who specialized in the Grinling Gibbons style of the late seventeenth century and who had a considerable talent for self-advertisement. His son W. H. Rogers became a well-known designer. Rogers was the first of many virtuosos who appealed to an unsophisticated taste for *trompe l'oeil* in wood. The storks and plants which supported a table by Morant shown at the Great Exhibition of 1851, and the dessert dishes by H. S. & D. Gass, also shown there, representing water plants at Kew Gardens with an exactitude reminiscent of those electrotype replicas of nature made possible by G. R. Elkington's patent electrical process of 1843, constitute an extension of the same taste, which could be handled with some elegance.

It was the use of apparently three dimensional plants and flowers to decorate carpets, wallpapers, and fabrics which aroused the ire of the painter William Dyce and the reformers associated with Henry Cole and the *Journal of Design*, which abhorred carpets with 'gigantic tropical plants, shown in high relief, and suggestive of anything but a level or plane'. That the *Journal of Design* should feel particularly strongly about such abuses was not surprising; its editor, Richard Redgrave, had taught botanical drawing at the School of Design from 1847 to 1848 and his *Manual of Design* (1876) spelled out his ideas on conventional rather than the imitative rendering of flowers and foliage.

The problem of the correct treatment of nature in ornament was one which exercised everyone seriously concerned with design in the 1850s. A. W. N. Pugin's *Floriated Ornament* (1849), although wholly Gothic in outlook, reached many of the same conclusions on the right disposition of leaves and flowers as did Owen Jones's *Grammar of Ornament* (1856). Plate XCVIII in his *Grammar*, illustrating 'the geometrical arrangement of flowers', was the work of Christopher Dresser, distinguished both as a botanist and a designer, who went on to develop an idiosyncratic ornamental style based on profound botanical knowledge, which he set out in various writings, including *The Art of Decorative Design* (1862).

A special problem faced the Gothic architect, who needed models for capitals and carvings. Early efforts to meet this need tended to be purely archaeological, such as the plates of Gothic ornament published by L. N. Cottingham in 1824, and J. K. Collings's *Gothic Ornament* (1848–53). However, Collings's later work, *Art Foliage* (1865), echoes the doctrines of design reformers such as Dresser in Gothic stiff-leaf foliage, with results more appropriate to the severity of Reformed Gothic than imitative naturalism.

John Ruskin, for whom the study of nature was all-important as the means to knowledge of God's revelation, and to whom J. M. W. Turner was the greatest

painter of the age precisely because of his knowledge of nature, was another advocate of its conventional treatment for ornament: 'all noble ornamentation is the expression of man's delight in God's work'. In the carved decoration of the Oxford University Museum, executed in the late 1850s by the O'Shea brothers from Dublin, directed by Ruskin and the architect, Benjamin Woodward, Ruskinian ideas found concrete expression, and a compromise was arranged between imitative Naturalism and conventional treatment which recalls the Pre-Raphaelite painters. Debased Ruskinian carving, which was disowned by Ruskin, later became the standard decoration for houses in the Gothic style, but the direct influence of the Oxford Museum in decorative art was limited; among the few exceptions is the carved decoration on some Gothic bookcases designed in about 1860 by the architect C. F. Hayward, for his friend John Jones, whose collection of *Dix-huitième* French art was left to the Victoria & Albert Museum in 1882.

The O'Shea brothers were not alone as specialist carvers of naturalistic ornament; Thomas Earp worked for S. S. Teulon at Shadwell Park, Norfolk (1855–60), Elvetham, Hampshire (1859–62), and Bestwood, Nottinghamshire (1862–4). The firm of Farmer & Brindley, London, usually executed Sir George Gilbert Scott's carving, and R. Bolton did some extraordinary work at Westholme, Cheltenham.

The Naturalistic style in ornament was contemporary with an increasing interest in plants and gardening, encouraged by such works as J. C. Loudon's *Gardener's Magazine* (1826–43) and the horticultural works of his wife, Jane Loudon. The biography of Sir Joseph Paxton is exemplary. Born in 1803, the son of a Bedfordshire farmer, he started as a gardener's boy, became Head Gardener to the Duke of Devonshire at Chatsworth, Derbyshire, in 1826, and published the *Horticultural Register and General Magazine* (1832–6), the *Magazine of Botany and Register of Flowering Plants* (1834–48), and other botanical and horticultural works. He gained an expertise in the design of glass buildings, which culminated in his design of the Crystal Palace of 1851, and worked as financier, landscape gardener, town planner, architect, and politician. It was probably in part due to Paxton's influence that the conservatory became such an essential adjunct to the country house. At the same time, influenced by Ruskin's attempt to elevate the landscape to the summit of the artistic hierarchy, there was a growing love of the countryside, which found expression in M. Birket Foster's *Pictures of English Landscape* (1864) and numerous similar albums.

The popularity of Sir Edwin Landseer's fancy pictures of animals represents another facet of Naturalism. Landseer was patronized by Prince Albert, and his paintings were reproduced on the ill-designed products of the Birmingham papier-mâché manufacturers. There was indeed a mid-nineteenth-century cult of the stag, of which Landseer was the major exponent, and at the 1851 Exhibition stags cropped up, to mention a few examples, on a bracket shown by the Gutta-Percha Company, on a cast-iron vase made by the Coalbrookdale Com-

pany, and on the Balmoral table-cloth by Messrs Hunt & Sons of Dunfermline, Scotland. Animals were successful in sculpture; the Grecian sculptor, Joseph Gott, had fancy animal groups in stock in his studio in Rome at his death in 1860. Naturalism also found expression in the use of unfamiliar natural materials, for example, in furniture made of coal, horns, antlers, and slate. Cast iron was another new material, first widely applied to furniture in the 1830s but, far from encouraging mechanistic functionalism, its manufacturers revelled in naturalistic flowers and leaves. A table designed by the sculptor, John Bell, and shown by the Coalbrookdale Company at the Paris Exhibition of 1855, represents an extreme; it was supported at each corner by realistic deerhounds whose heads projected somewhat impractically above its surface.

At the London Exhibition of 1862 most of the wilder excesses of Naturalism were absent. But Naturalism remained a dominant form of ornament. Imitative Naturalism decorated Copeland's Neo-classical ceramics, Gillows's Renaissance sideboard, designed by Jefferson, and Blashfield's Renaissance terracotta ornaments. English wild flowers occurred on lace by Debenham & Freebody, and Howell & James, while Mappin & Company showed a flower vase constructed of bulrushes. Palissy ware by Mintons combined imitative Naturalism with antiquarianism and Renaissance Revival. Nature conventionalized covered Tayler Harry & Company's Kamptulicon (a patent floor covering), Sir George Gilbert Scott's choir screen for Hereford Cathedral, made by Skidmore's Art-Manufactures, Scott, Cuthbertson & Company's wallpapers, influenced by Pugin, Walters & Sons' silks, and Bone's bookbindings. Owen Jones's binding in relief leather for his *Victorian Psalter*, chromolithographed by Day & Sons, was a *tour de force*, a synthesis of conventional and imitative treatment of foliage. Later in the 1860s Jones was to use naturalistic ornament for his Oriental Courts in the South Kensington Museum, London, while Edward Poynter mingled Naturalism with Japanese influence in the Museum's Grill Room.

Naturalism, defined as an independent style, reached its peak in the early 1850s, but it continued to be popular into the 1860s. Naturalism in a wider sense was important throughout the High Victorian period, and its importance as the principal basis of ornament in an age which considered ornament as synonymous with art cannot be exaggerated. That the study of nature had moral overtones increased its attraction to both designers and their public.

47

Gas jet of gilt brass with blue and white pottery flowers, manufactured by R. W. Winfield, the
design registered in 1848. Winfield was the leading Birmingham manufacturer of brass beds. In
1846 he was producing curtain pole ends incorporating glass flowers, similar to this gas jet; they
were designed by W. C. Aitken, a superintendent of Winfield's Cambridge Street Works. In 1851
Queen Victoria bought from Winfields a three-light gas bracket in bronze with lilies and a statuette
of Dorothea in Parian porcelain.

48

Dish, Staffordshire earthenware, about 1855. This dish is in the style of Bernard Palissy, who manufactured 'rustic' wares incorporating snails, lizards, snakes, and fish, from about 1548. These were imitated by Charles Avisseau of Tours in the early 1840s and by Mintons of Stoke-on-Trent in the 1850s. In 1852 a two volume life of Palissy by Henry Morley (1822–94) was published and he became a Victorian cult-figure, admired both as self-made man and as persecuted Protestant.

49

Vase, porcelain, by Minton & Co., Stoke-on-Trent, about 1859. This vase was purchased by the South Kensington Museum (now Victoria & Albert Museum) in 1859 for £26 5s. The delicate naturalism of its low relief flowers and grasses, white on a celadon green ground, may have been influenced by the Wedgwood jasper wares still being produced in the 1850s. It is in marked contrast to the often gross handling of natural forms on contemporary stoneware jugs.

50

Plate, porcelain, manufactured by Minton & Co., Stoke-on-Trent and painted by John Latham, 1862. This plate was purchased by the South Kensington Museum (now Victoria & Albert Museum) in 1862 for 14s 8d. Latham had worked for the Coalport factory in the 1820s. The butterflies on the plate reflect a wide-spread Victorian interest, promoted by pundits such as the Reverend F. O. Morris (1810–93), anti-vivisectionist, opponent of Darwin, and author of *A History of British Butterflies* (1853).

VI

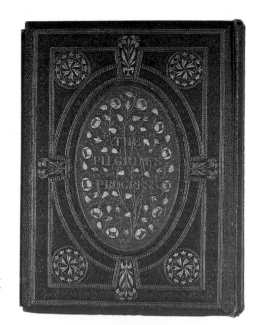

VII

VIII

VI   Victorian Neo-Classicism
Wine jug, silver, by Charles Reily and George Storer, London, 1840 to 1841. Reily and Storer, descended from a wine-label maker of the 1730s, Sandylands Drinkwater, worked in a wide variety of styles. This jug, based on an antique Italo-Greek oenochoe is a typical specimen of the Etruscan taste which continued to be fashionable into the late 1860s. The engraved figures are probably derived from engravings after Greek vase paintings.

VII   Naturalism
Binding of John Bunyan, *Pilgrim's Progress* (1861), by Leighton, Sons & Hodge. This edition, with illustrations by J. D. Watson (1832–92) engraved by the Brothers Dalziel, was highly successful. The *Art Journal* commented: 'A rich binding of the fashionable *Magenta* colour is an additional attraction presented by the book'. Numerous illustrated editions of *Pilgrim's Progress* were published in the mid-nineteenth century.

VIII   Naturalism
Table of inlaid marble designed by J. Randall and made by Samuel Birley of Ashford, Derbyshire, about 1862. This table won Birley a medal in both the Furniture and Mining Classes of the London 1862 Exhibition; it was purchased by the South Kensington Museum (now Victoria & Albert Museum) for no less than £240. The Derbyshire marble industry is said to have commenced in 1748. It was much encouraged by the sixth Duke of Devonshire (1790–1858), who allowed craftsmen to study his collection of Florentine marble inlay at Chatsworth.

51
Framed panel of porcelain by Copeland, about 1847. The panel is painted with orchidaceous flowers, a symptom of another Victorian interest, shared by many scientists, including the great botanist, John Lindley (1799–1865), the founder of modern orchidology, and Charles Darwin (1809–82), who in 1862 published a book on the fertilization of orchids by insects, a supplemental treatise to his *Origin of Species* (1859).

52
Four glazed tiles made by Maw & Co. at the Benthall Works, near Coalbrookdale, Shropshire, after 1853. The decoration of these tiles, a trilobite and various crystalline effects, probably reflects the interest in geology of George Maw, who was a keen supporter of the Museum of Practical Geology, the original owner of the tiles. Its 1875 catalogue included as an appendix a systematic list of native clays and their ceramic utility, prepared by Maw.

57

Design for a wallpaper by Owen Jones (1809–74) for Jackson & Graham, 1860. It well illustrates Proposition XIII in Jones's *Grammar of Ornament* (1856): 'Flowers or other natural objects should not be used as ornaments, but conventional representations founded upon them sufficiently suggestive to convey the intended image to the mind, without destroying the unity of the object they are employed to decorate. *Universally obeyed in the best periods of Art, equally violated when Art declines'.*

58

Design for tiles in the Grill Room, South Kensington Museum (now Victoria & Albert Museum), watercolour on photograph, by E. J. Poynter (1836–1919), about 1869. These tiles were painted by the female students of the South Kensington Museum porcelain class. Poynter had in 1864 designed a mosaic of Phidias for the South Court of the Museum and in 1870 presented a scheme, unexecuted, to decorate its Lecture Theatre. His Grill Room also included an Anglo-Japanese iron stove dated 1866.

professional than Burges, and his architecture, although using the same Reformed Gothic repertoire, displayed a more amiable and picturesque variety. Another contemporary, G. F. Bodley, like Street and White a pupil of Scott, worked in the 1850s and early 1860s in the Reformed manner, using simple bare forms, plate tracery, as approved by Ruskin, and sharp polychromy. In the late 1860s he reverted to a graceful fourteenth-century style, consciously rejecting the severe forms of his youth. James Brooks, two years older than Bodley, remained faithful to large, simple forms in a series of monumental brick town churches dating from the 1860s to the 1880s. J. L. Pearson, one of the older generation born in 1817, developed from Puginian beginnings in the late 1840s, through a Reformed phase to a refined – if sometimes bland – later manner. His masterpiece was Truro Cathedral, Cornwall, begun in 1880. His St Augustine's, Kilburn, London (1870), is the perfect illustration of the moment of transition between High Victorian toughness and Late Victorian refinement.

A younger group of architects born in the early 1830s came into prominence in about 1860; they all used the repertoire of Reformed Gothic, though not all of them remained faithful to it. They include, in order of seniority, C. F. Hayward, Alfred Waterhouse, Philip Webb, Richard Norman Shaw, E. W. Godwin, William Morris (who never practised as an architect) and W. E. Nesfield.

Each of these architects was involved in the 1860s in the design of furniture and decoration, and much of the former was painted in accordance with the early French Gothic models admired by William Burges, and first imitated in his 1855 design of an organ case for Lille Cathedral, France. Models for church furniture had been supplied by Butterfield and others in the late 1840s and the 1850s, and the ecclesiological repertoire of revealed construction, chamfering, stump columns, and geometrical inlay was converted to secular use. The new style of furniture received its first conspicuous public showing in the Mediaeval Court of the London Exhibition of 1862, organised by Burges, but by the mid 1860s commercial manufacturers were copying its motifs in more superficially decorative, but less architecturally pure, combinations. The two best-known designers were Charles Bevan and B. J. Talbert, whose *Gothic Forms Applied to Furniture* (1867) presented models for imitation.

Metalwork, tiles, and other forms of decoration in the Reformed Gothic style followed a similar progression to furniture – in the 1850s, the province of architects, and made to order, preponderantly for ecclesiastical use; in the 1860s, produced by commercial manufacturers and designed by professional designers.

Although its formal innovations are the most striking aspect of Reformed Gothic, it did not lack an archaeological and theoretical basis. A committed periodical, *The Ecclesiologist*, has already been mentioned. There were also technical treatises including F. A. Paley's *A Manual of Gothic Mouldings* (1845), Edmund Sharpe's *A Treatise on the Rise and Fall of Decorated Window Tracery in England* (1849), and R. W. Billings's *The Power of Form Applied to Geometric Tracery*

IX

X

104

IX   The Reformed Gothic Style
Cabinet, designed by William Burges (1827–81) for H. G. Yatman, 1858. This cabinet, made by
Harland & Fisher with figure painting by E. J. Poynter (1836–1919), was shown at the London
Architectural Exhibition in 1859 and at the London 1862 International Exhibition. The first major
monument of Victorian Gothic painted furniture it was strongly influenced by thirteenth-century
French armoires at Bayeux and Noyon. Burges had examined the one at Noyon in 1853;
Viollet-le-Duc (1814–79) published both in 1858.

X   The Reformed Gothic Style
Design for the east end of St Mary, Whitechapel, by Ernest Claude Lee (1846–90), 1878. Lee, a
pupil of Colonel R. W. Edis (1839–1927), who worked mainly in a middle-brow Queen Anne
style, was himself strongly influenced by William Burges and often collaborated, as here, with
Burges's chief artist, H. R. Lonsdale. The combination of rich sculpture, on the reredos, vigorous
polychromy, on walls and altar-frontal, and bold geometry in form and ornament are typically
Burgesian.

(1851). Such works were more than archaeological, they presented the possibility of new, formal combinations based on the knowledge of correct principles. The writings of Eugène Viollet-le-Duc increased the knowledge of Gothic structures and techniques. In Oxford, John Henry Parker, publisher and author, took over the mantle of John Britton for a more exacting generation. Continental models were published in, for example, R. Norman Shaw's *Architectural Sketches from the Continent* (1858), W. Eden Nesfield's *Specimens of Mediaeval Architecture* (1862), and G. E. Street's *Some Accounts of Gothic Architecture in Spain* (1865). And in 1872 C. L. Eastlake summarized progress in his *A History of the Gothic Revival*. In the early 1870s it must have seemed that the battle for Reformed Gothic was being won; it was not the preponderant style, but it was the style for great national buildings – Street's Law Courts, London (1868–81), Scott's St Pancras Hotel, London (1868–74), Alfred Waterhouse's Natural History Museum in South Kensington, London (1873–81), and begun as early as 1859, Thomas Fuller and Chilion Jones's Parliament Buildings in Ottawa.

But appearances were deceptive. Committed Goths were turning to more elegant later models and many of the most gifted younger architects were making eclectic use of eighteenth-century models. The Reformed Gothic style, in fact, ceased effectively to innovate by the late 1860s. For a short period, however, it had been a living style, with qualities of strength, conviction, and coherence all too rare in English architecture. It evaporated because the moral impetus for reform had petered out, and because the process of re-forming the language of thirteenth-century Gothic to fit the needs and materials of nineteenth-century England had produced a style too severe and radical to suit English taste for the comfortable and picturesque in architecture. A glimpse of how radical the Reformed Gothic style was may be gained from T. G. Jackson's memory of the young Thomas Garner (later a partner of G. F. Bodley) falling into raptures over a hansom cab because it was 'so truthful, so – so – so – mediaeval'.

62
Davenport, designed by Charles Bevan and made by Marsh & Jones of Leeds in about 1864. A design for a similar davenport by Bevan was published first in the *Building News* (1865), and later in the *House—Furnisher and Decorator* (1872). It was strongly influenced by a desk designed by John Pollard Seddon (1827–1906) shown at the London 1862 Exhibition. The Victoria & Albert Museum possesses a piano close to the *Building News* davenport design and drawings for both.

73
Northampton Town Hall, 1864, from a photograph of about 1870. Northampton Town Hall was the first major building by Edward William Godwin (1833–86), built as the outcome of a competition. Eastlake, in *A History of the Gothic Revival* (1872), detected that Godwin had been 'strongly influenced by the prevalent taste for Italian Gothic' and by Ruskin. Godwin had indeed read Ruskin's *Stones of Venice* (1851–3) shortly before the competition.

74
Rugby School Chapel, designed by William Butterfield (1814–1900), from a
late-nineteenth-century photograph. The Chapel was built from 1870 to 1872; Butterfield added
mosaics in 1882. His patron at Rugby, Frederick Temple (1821–1902), became Archbishop of
Canterbury in 1897. The interior of Rugby Chapel, cream and pink sandstone columns and
patterned brick walls, exemplifies Butterfield's High Victorian interest in colour, which reflects
Ruskin's advocacy of polychromy.

75

Tower House, Melbury Road, London, from a photograph of about 1880. Tower House was designed by William Burges (1827–81) in 1875 as 'a model residence of the thirteenth century' for his own use, and was built from 1876 to 1878. Described in 1925 by W. R. Lethaby (1857–1931) as 'massive, learned, glittering, amazing', Tower House is a paradigm of Reformed Gothic strength and clarity in its exterior, in contrast to the fantastic elaboration of its interior.

76
The Grimshaw Building, Sunderland, about 1875, from a late-ninteenth-century photograph.
This vigorous assemblage of Reformed Gothic motifs, the decoration executed in terracotta, is
typical of the commercialization of the style from the late 1860s onwards. Ruskin referred to such
buildings as 'accursed Frankenstein monsters of, *in*directly, my own making' and lamented that
'there is scarcely a public-house near the Crystal Palace but sells its gin and bitters under
pseudo-Venetian capitals'.

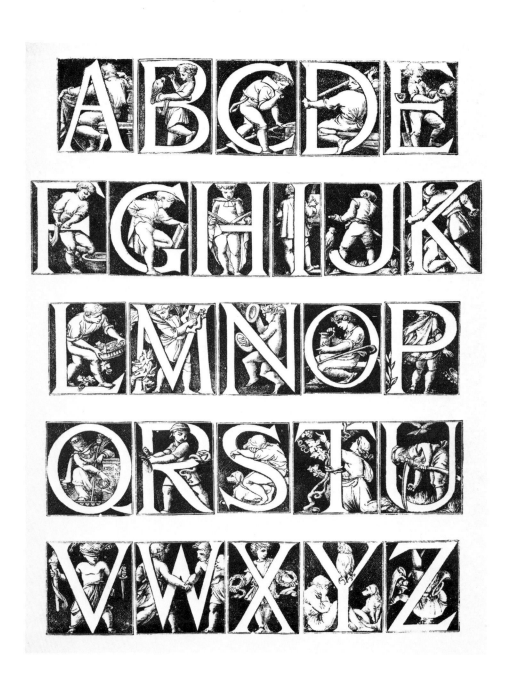

77
Alphabet designed by Godfrey Sykes (1825–66), 1864. This alphabet was designed for the Centre Refreshment Room of the South Kensington Museum (now Victoria & Albert Museum). The letters were executed in glazed earthenware by Minton, Hollins & Co. from 1867, and published in *The South Kensington Museum* (1881). They were influenced by initials in use in Venice in the early sixteenth century, and by others designed by Hans Holbein for Basle printers in about 1530. Kate Greenaway (1846–1901) designed a later version with winsome children in William Mavor, *The English Spelling Book* (1885).

6

The Renaissance Revival

That taste for the picturesque which encouraged the revival of Elizabethan and
Jacobean architecture – 'English Renaissance' as the style was called – also
prompted the invention, in the early nineteenth century, of an Italianate style
culled from the buildings shown in the paintings of Claude Lorrain and Nicolas
Poussin. The later adoption of the urban palazzo as a model was accompanied by
the revival of the whole Renaissance repertoire of ornament, both from Italy and
northern Europe. In fact the Renaissance Revival comprised many revivals, rarely
pursued with the moral fervour aroused by Gothic, the Christian style *par excellence*
in the eyes of its Roman and Anglo-Catholic propagandists, but offering a
luxuriant choice of motifs and materials which reconciled most architects and
designers, and their clients, to paganism.

John Nash's Cronkhill, Shropshire (1802) is the earliest monument of the
Italianate villa style, more expressively called the 'Rural Italian Style' by Robert
Kerr in his *The English Gentleman's House* (1865). In the first quarter of the
nineteenth century, it received the approval of the two greatest connoisseurs of the
age, Thomas Hope and William Beckford. From 1818 to 1823 Thomas Hope,
with the assistance of the architect William Atkinson, transformed his conventional mid-eighteenth-century mansion, The Deepdene, Surrey, into what
J. C. Loudon called in 1833 'the finest example in England of an Italian villa,
united with the grounds by architectural appendages'. From 1825 to 1826 William
Beckford's architect, H. E. Goodridge, created in Lansdown Tower, Bath, a
synthesis of refined Grecian details with an irregular Italian plan and outline. The
sublimely Gothic Fonthill Abbey, Wiltshire (1796–1807), designed for Beckford
by James Wyatt, although stylistically dissimilar, shared the same flexible plan and
varied outline. Goodridge's own house, Montebello, Bath (1828–30) moved even
closer to the final Italianate mode. This was fully developed in the 1830s, and
Charles Parker's *Villa Rustica* (1832–41) epitomizes the style. It was not only
applied to the rustic villa, but also to country houses on the grandest scale, most
notably Barry's enlargement of Trentham, Staffordshire (1834–41) for the Duke
of Sutherland. Less palatial, but even more influential, was the collaboration of
the Prince Consort and the builder/architect, Thomas Cubitt, in the rebuilding of
Osborne House, Isle of Wight (1844–8), as a summer residence for the Royal
family. By his example in Belgravia, which he developed from 1820s to the 1840s,

Cubitt was also largely instrumental in making Italianate detail executed in stucco the standard finish of the town house of the 1850s.

The origins of a more academic Renaissance Revival (for 'Rural Italian' was Renaissance only in the sketchiest sense) have received little attention, although even in a building of 1769 to 1778, George Dance's Newgate Gaol, London, the influence of Giulio Romano's house at Mantua and the Pitti Palace in Florence is visible. Indeed, Sir Charles Barry's Traveller's Club in Pall Mall, London (1829–32), a Florentine palazzo with no Grecian details, appears almost as a *deus ex machina*; certainly it was made to seem so by W. H. Leeds's *The Travellers' Club House . . . Accompanied by an Essay on the Present State of Architectural Study and the Revival of the Italian Style* (1839). Barry's later Manchester Athenaeum (1837–9), another palazzo, was followed by his greatest achievement in this mode, the Reform Club (1838–40) in Pall Mall, next to the Travellers' Club. It was based on Giuliano da San Gallo's Farnese Palace in Rome. This series of club buildings set the pattern for later club architects, for example, Sydney Smirke, whose Carlton Club, London (1847) was based on Jacopo Sansovino's Library of St Mark in Venice. Barry later used the palazzo for a domestic palace, Bridgwater House, London (completed 1854), which was even larger than the Reform Club. Barry's handling of Renaissance detail tended to become broader, more opulent and, it must be admitted, coarser, as the century advanced. In contrast Sir John Soane's late work, the State Paper Office, London (1829–33), is a severe sixteenth-century mannerist exercise, derived from Vignola. C. R. Cockerell, Soane's successor as architect to the Bank of England, London (1788–1833), was an even more refined manipulator of mannerist motifs exhibited in, for example, his branch offices for the Bank of England in Bristol and Liverpool and his Sun Life Assurance Office, London (1839–42). Prestige commercial buildings of all kinds were usually built in a Renaissance style throughout the High Victorian period; and a simplified version was often used for more utilitarian purposes, as in Charles Fowler's Hungerford Market, London (1831–3) or Edward l'Anson's Royal Exchange Buildings, London (1842–4).

Interior decoration in the Renaissance manner was rare in the 1830s, although Barry's Travellers' Club contained Raphaelesque painting by Sang, who later executed similar decoration in George Basevi and Sydney Smirke's Palladian Conservative Club, London (1843–5) and in James Bunning's Coal Exchange, London (1847–9). In the 1840s, influenced by the personal taste of Prince Albert, the Renaissance style became de facto that of the establishment. The Prince's decorative adviser was Ludwig Gruner, who helped to organize the Garden Pavilion built in the grounds of Buckingham Palace in 1844, and published *The Decoration of the Garden Pavilion in the Grounds of Buckingham Palace* in 1846. Gruner also supplied coloured tracings of Renaissance ornament to the School of Design, produced decorative designs for the Great Exhibition of 1851, and issued *Description of the Plates of Fresco Decorations and Stuccoes of Churches and Palaces in*

Italy in the fifteenth and sixteenth centuries (1854).

The Prince also patronized William Dyce (most Nazarene and therefore most Raphaelite of English painters), who became Director of the School of Design at Somerset House, London, in 1838, and remained so until 1843. The exhibition in Westminster Hall that year, of the competition of designs for the proposed fresco decorations of the New Palace of Westminster, was organized under the Prince's chairmanship, and was the occasion for lengthy discussions and controversy on the appropriate style and technique for the revival of fresco, in which C. L. Eastlake, whom the Prince had chosen as Secretary to his Royal Commission, played a major role.

Another friend of the Prince, Sir Henry Cole, was in effective control of the School of Design, London, from about 1847 onwards. Cole was a Dyce supporter and, in the role of 'Felix Summerly', a promoter of model designs by Renaissance-oriented artists such as the sculptor, John Bell, and the painter, Richard Redgrave. Redgrave generally acted as a supporter in Cole's struggles with the School of Design, which culminated in the creation of the Department of Practical Art in 1852. In 1845 Alfred Stevens was appointed to teach 'drawing and painting, ornament, geometrical drawing and modelling' at the School of Design.

Stevens was a sculptor and designer of genius, with a command of High Renaissance forms unparalleled among his contemporaries, and even after his resignation in 1848 he exercised great influence on a large group of pupils and admirers, who promoted the use of the Renaissance style for decoration. Stevens gained first-hand experience of decorative design at a practical level by working for the iron-founders, H. E. Hoole & Company, and other Sheffield firms, and by designing ceramics for Mintons. Stevens also executed Renaissance decoration in Deysbrook, Liverpool (1847) and at Lewis Vulliamy's Dorchester House, London (1851–7), and was responsible for several important unexecuted schemes, including one for the decoration of the Reading Room, British Museum, London (in collaboration with Sydney Smirke). Godfrey Sykes was Steven's most influential disciple; he designed much of the terracotta and ceramic ornament in the South Kensington Museum, with whose architect, Francis Fowke, he collaborated closely. Terracotta decoration was also promoted by Gruner; his *The Terracotta Architecture of North Italy* appeared in 1867.

From 1850 to 1855 Gottfried Semper, the greatest German art theorist of the nineteenth century and an ardent supporter of the Renaissance Revival, was in London. He became friendly with Prince Albert, taught at the School of Design, designed the Duke of Wellington's funeral car, and wrote for Henry Cole's *Journal of Design and Manufactures*. Semper also designed for commercial firms; a cabinet executed by Holland & Sons, the leading London cabinet-makers, was shown at the Paris Exhibition of 1855 and purchased five years later by the South Kensington Museum. Semper was the most distinguished foreign designer to have worked in London, but there were many others and they all encouraged the

Renaissance Revival: Léon Arnoux, the French Art Director of Mintons, pioneered their Victorian Majolica; and Mintons also employed Émile Jeannest, Carrier Belleuse, and Hugues Protat. Protat designed the buffet (1853) for Alscot Park, Warwickshire, executed by the virtuoso carver William Cookes of Warwick, and Jackson & Graham of London showed at the Paris Exhibition of 1855 a cabinet designed by Eugène Prignot, another Frenchman. Benjamin Schlick, a Danish architect trained in Paris, worked for the Birmingham goldsmiths' firm of Elkingtons, the pioneers of electrotypes, in the Renaissance style. Elkingtons also employed Gruner, Léonard Morel-Ladeuil, and A. A. Willms, Morel-Ladeuil's master. Antoine Vechte worked for the London goldsmiths Hunt & Roskell, and many of his designs were reproduced in electrotype by Elkingtons.

The influence of these foreign designers was reflected in the much greater sophistication in the handling of Renaissance ornament displayed in the London International Exhibition of 1862 as opposed to the Great Exhibition of 1851. Even the 1862 building, by Francis Fowke, was Renaissance in style, as were its painted decorations by J. G. Crace, the leading interior decorator of the age. H. H. Armstead and Frank Hunt of Hunt & Roskell, R. W. Binns of Worcester Porcelain Works, Alfred Stevens for Mintons, and Matthew Digby Wyatt for Maw & Company, the tile manufacturers in Shropshire, are among the leading English designers of Renaissance ornament whose work stood up to foreign comparison.

It is a measure of the entrenchment of the Renaissance Revival in the taste of the establishment that Lord Palmerston was able to win the battle of the styles between Classic and Gothic and that, as a result, Sir George Gilbert Scott's Italian design of 1861 for the Foreign Office, London, was built instead of his original Gothic design of 1856. Even a Goth like William Burges was persuaded to work in the Renaissance style in Worcester College Chapel, Oxford (1864). In 1872 Burges was the surprise choice of the Dean and Chapter to finish the decoration of St Paul's Cathedral, but his scheme was not executed. (Alfred Steven's involvement with the cathedral authorities from 1860 onwards was almost equally fruitless.)

However, the Renaissance Revival was rarely used for ecclesiastical purposes; it was a fundamentally secular style, which affected the design of secular buildings of all kinds – clubs, offices, town halls, hotels, and houses. There was rarely much academic rigour in its application and High Victorian Renaissance Revival merged imperceptibly into Late Victorian Free Renaissance, which often overlapped with the Queen Anne style. This flexibility probably accounts for the widespread use and popularity of the style. It has to be admitted that coarseness is a frequent attribute of Renaissance Revival design, and that few architects and designers, apart from Barry, Cockerell, and Stevens, handled the style with any real power. But the Renaissance Revival did produce many works whose refinement of decorative detail and unsurpassed skill in the handling of rich materials render them worthy of admiration, even in an age dominated by the dogma of functionalism.

78
Panel, oak by James Osmond, 1870. This panel received a prize at the London Workmen's International Exhibition of 1870 and from the Society of Arts in the same year. It was later shown at the London 1872 International Exhibition and at the 1888 Arts and Crafts Exhibition. This success was due to a synthesis of technical brilliance, refined Renaissance grotesque ornament, and Naturalism.

79
Ewer, electrotype, by Elkington, Mason & Co., 1852. This ewer was purchased by the Museum of
Ornamental Art (now Victoria & Albert Museum) in 1854 for £9 9s. It is adapted from a ewer by
François Briot, a celebrated French pewterer who worked in Montbéliard from 1579. His refined
mannerist style inspired imitations by contemporaries, in both pottery and silver, and was greatly
admired by Victorian designers.

80

Sketch model for a fire-dog, by Alfred Stevens (1817–75), about 1855. This fire-dog was
manufactured by Messrs. Hoole of Sheffield and shown together with their 'Pluto Dog' stove at
the London 1862 Exhibition. Stevens was engaged by Henry Hoole in 1850 and repaid Hoole's
generous patronage with arrogance and disloyalty. Nonetheless the products of their collaboration,
which ended in 1857, were acclaimed at the London 1851, Paris 1855 and London 1862
Exhibitions.

81
Vase, porcelain, by Minton & Co., Stoke-on-Trent, about 1857. This vase was purchased by the
South Kensington Museum (now Victoria & Albert Museum) in 1857 for £21. Its grotesque
decoration was designed by Silas Rice, who worked for Wedgwoods after 1860, and painted by
Thomas Allen, who had been trained at the London School of Design from 1852 to 1854. The
design reflects the influence of Alfred Stevens (1817–75).

130

82

Ewer, earthenware, modelled by Hamlet Bourne and manufactured by Minton & Co.,
Stoke-on-Trent, 1858. This ewer, together with a stand, was purchased by the South Kensington
Museum (now Victoria & Albert Museum) in 1859 for £3 10s. It is copied from a ewer attributed
to the sixteenth-century French potter Bernard Palissy from the Soulages collection which had
been on view in the Museum of Ornamental Art, Marlborough House, from 1856 to 1857 and was
acquired by the South Kensington Museum in 1860 through a public subscription to which
Herbert Minton (1793–1858) had contributed £1,000.

83

Candlestick, earthenware, by Minton & Co., Stoke-on-Trent, 1859. This polychrome candlestick was purchased by the South Kensington Museum (now Victoria & Albert Museum) in 1859 for £4 5s. Its form is freely adapted from a model attributed to the sixteenth-century French potter, Bernard Palissy, and nicely represents the Victorian taste for and command of Renaissance Grotesque ornament, in which naturalistic elements are often prominent.

84
Panel of four tiles, earthenware, by Maw & Co. of the Benthall Works, near Coalbrookdale,
Shropshire, about 1871. These tiles were presented by the manufacturers to the Museum of
Practical Geology in 1871, as examples of modern Majolica ware. The relief heads may be
influenced by those on a Palissy ware cistern in the Fountaine collection illustrated in Joseph
Marryat, *A History of Pottery and Porcelain* (1857) and acquired by the South Kensington Museum
(now Victoria & Albert Museum) in 1885.

85

Binding for *Bible Events* (second series), published by Joseph Cundall in 1844, with six illustrations after 'Raffaele'. The first series of Bible Events (1843) had illustrations after Holbein. Both formed part of *Felix Summerly's Home Treasury*, some twenty children's books edited from 1843 to 1846 by Henry Cole (1808–82), whose illustrators included Richard Redgrave, J. C. Horsley, J. H. Townsend and John Linnell. Cole's printer, Charles Whittingham (1795–1876), who took over the Chiswick Press from his uncle in 1840, revived the eighteeenth-century Caslon typeface for the series.

86
Binding for *Illustrated Ditties of the Olden Time* (Brighton, 1850), green cloth embossed in gold.
Traditional Nursery Songs (1843), the second volume in *Felix Summerly's Home Treasury*, had
encouraged a new appreciation of nursery rhymes. *Illustrated Ditties*, published by Robert
Folthorp, comprised a selection with a naturalistic title-page and lithographed illustrations. The
strapwork ornament on its cover was probably intended to recall an Elizabethan Renaissance
'Olden Time'.

87
Details of the decoration of Dorchester House, London, by Alfred Stevens (1817–75), about 1860. The prominent crouching caryatid is a study for the dining room chimneypiece, now in the Victoria & Albert Museum. Dorchester House was designed by Lewis Vulliamy (1791–1871) for Robert Stainer Holford (1808–92), a collector, gardener and landed magnate whose fortune derived from shares in the New River Company. Stevens was engaged to decorate the dining room in 1856; it was incomplete at his death.

XI

XII

137

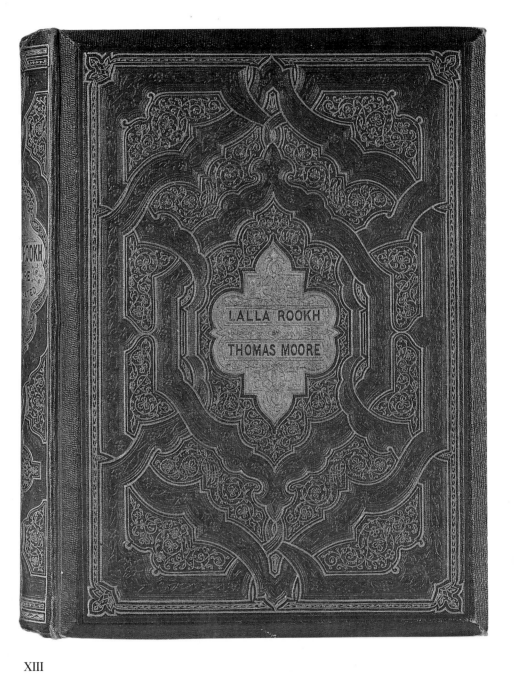

XIII

XI   The Renaissance Revival
Card case, electrotype silvered and parcel-gilt, made by Elkington, Mason & Co., designed by George Clark Stanton (1832–94), 1852. This card case was purchased by the Museum of Ornamental Art (now Victoria & Albert Museum) for £1 10s in 1854. It was later shown at the Paris 1855 and London 1862 Exhibitions. Stanton studied at the Birmingham School of Design; in 1855 he moved to Edinburgh where he was active as sculptor and painter.

XII   The Renaissance Revival
Tazza and cover, bone china, by Minton & Co. of Stoke-on-Trent, painted by Stephen Lawton, about 1860. This tazza was purchased by the South Kensington Museum (now Victoria & Albert Museum) for £15 in 1860. Stephen Lawton specialized in the painting of imitations of sixteenth-century Limoges enamels, produced by Mintons from about 1856. This tazza is comparable in form to one executed by Pierre Reymond of Limoges for Linhard Tucher of Nuremberg in 1558.

XIII   The Exotic
Binding of Thomas Moore, *Lalla Rookh: An Oriental Romance* (1861), purple cloth embossed in gold and silver. This elaborate edition includes five pages of Persian ornament mainly taken from manuscripts at the British Museum and East India House: these were designed by T. Sulman who was probably also responsible for the binding. Sulman earlier designed an Islamic style binding for *Sakoontala* (1855) published by Stephen Austin of Hertford and is likely to have designed the similar binding to Austin's *The Gulistan of Sadi* (1852).

88

Osborne House, Isle of Wight, built from 1845 to 1851, from a photograph of about 1860. The
Osborne estate was bought by Queen Victoria and Prince Albert in 1844, as an island retreat. The
Prince collaborated closely with his builder, Thomas Cubitt (1788–1855), on the Italianate
rebuilding of the house. Its final composition, with a pavilion added to the old house to
accommodate the Royal family, recalls Trentham Park, remodelled from 1834 by Sir Charles
Barry (1795–1860) for the Duchess of Sutherland, Mistress of the Robes to Queen Victoria.

89
The Renaissance Court at the Crystal Palace, Sydenham, designed by Sir Matthew Digby Wyatt
(1820–77) in 1853, from a photograph of about 1860. This view includes, in the foreground, a
fountain from the Doge's Palace in Venice, surmounted by the Verrocchio fountain figure from
the Palazzo Vecchio in Florence and, in the background, the tomb effigy of Robert Legendre in
the Louvre above an altar frontal from the Certosa, Pavia.

buildings as 'toys in architecture': nonetheless, he had visited China, and *Designs* is significant as one of the earliest works to have published accurate representations of Chinese buildings. Chambers's pagoda at the Royal Botanic Gardens at Kew, Surrey (1762) is one of the major surviving monuments of mid-eighteenth-century chinoiserie, and the fashion for the *jardin anglo-chinois*, which provided an excuse for Chinese pavilions all over Europe for the rest of the century, was partly inspired by his *Dissertation on Oriental Gardening* (1760). A Chinese Fishing Temple at Virginia Water, Surrey (1826), designed by Sir Jeffry Wyatville and executed by Frederick Crace for George IV, is one of the late wonders of this style (in 1860 it was repaired by Teulon, one of the most *outré* of Victorian Goths!).

Already at Kew, Chambers had designed an alhambra and a mosque, and as early as 1750 a pavilion in the 'Old Moorish Taste' was erected there. Indian or Moorish influence was fragmentary until the travels of William Hodges were recorded in *Select Views of India* (1785–8) and Thomas and William Daniell published *Oriental Scenery* (1794–1808). The first serious monument in Indian style was Sezincote House, Gloucestershire, designed by Samuel Pepys Cockerell in about 1805; Thomas Daniell was responsible for a number of garden buildings at Sezincote in the Indian style. Daniell also influenced William Porden's Dome at Brighton (1803) and Humphry Repton's illustrations in his *Designs for the Pavilion at Brighton* (1808), both in the Indian style. When Brighton Pavilion received its final form (1815–21), it was in accordance with designs by John Nash; its Hindu exterior and chinoiserie interior constituted not only the greatest monument of exoticism, but also a permanent reminder of George IV's extravagance which lent unfavourable associations to any wild flights into the exotic in the eyes of many Victorians.

In fact, apart from occasional garden and commercial buildings, Chinese was not a common architectural style in the mid-nineteenth century. Nor was the Moorish style much used, being largely reserved for the interiors of smoking-rooms and the exteriors of Turkish baths. But there was a widespread romantic taste for literature on Moorish and Indian themes, typified by Thomas Moore's *Lalla Rookh* (1817). One product of the romantic movement was Owen Jones. The son of a Welsh furrier and antiquary he travelled widely in Europe and the Near East in the early 1830s. An outcome of these travels was his magnificent chromolithographed *Plans, elevations, sections and details of the Alhambra* (1836–45), a landmark in the publication of Islamic architecture. Another result was a considerable facility in design in the Moorish style, which he used in a few houses, in a series of lavishly illuminated books, and in decorative design in every medium. His *Grammar of Ornament* (1856) surveyed all historic styles and also exotic ornament, with a strong bias in favour of Islamic styles. Its authority and scholarship is all the more evident when Jones's illustrations are compared to those in Richard Brown's *Domestic Architecture* (1841), an earlier universal compendium. Brown illustrated 'A Persian Pavilion', 'A Chinese Residence',

'A Burmese Palatial Hall of Assembly', 'An Oriental Pavilion', and 'A Morisco-Spanish Palatial Building' with comments on decoration and furniture as uncertain as his captions.

The belief that all nations could combine and understand one another through trade was symbolized by displays at the major exhibitions from every part of the world. In the Great Exhibition of 1851, for instance, there was blackwood furniture, shawls, and metalwork from India; Owen Jones commented that the Indian exhibits amazed everyone 'by the presence of so much unity of design, so much skill and judgment in its application, with so much elegance and refinement in the execution'. Chinese lacquer, often of low quality, continued to be imported as it had been in the eighteenth century, and the manufacturers of papier mâché in Birmingham continued to 'japan' their wares, although occasionally now Moorish designs were used. An exhibition of Japanese applied art was held in London in 1854, and purchases were made by Sir Henry Cole and Richard Redgrave. This exhibition was probably one result of the expedition made by the American Commodore Perry (1794–1858) in November 1852 which initiated the opening of Japan to the West. But Japanese influence was rare in the 1850s, although Mintons produced some remarkable Chinese-influenced ceramics which were shown at the London International Exhibition of 1862.

Also at the 1862 Exhibition a Japanese Court, organized by Sir Rutherford Alcock, the first representative of the Crown at Edo (Tokyo) in 1859, stimulated an unprecedented interest in Japanese art and design. One of those who were impressed was William Burges, the Gothic architect, in whose view 'these hitherto unknown barbarians appear not only to know all that the Middle Ages knew but in some respects are beyond them and us as well'. E. W. Godwin, at that date also a Goth, reacted by using Japanese prints to decorate his home in Bristol, Gloucestershire. The contents of the Japanese department of the exhibition were sold off, some to enthusiasts such as Godwin and the designer, Christopher Dresser, by the Oriental Department of Messrs Farmer & Rogers, whose manager for twelve years, Arthur Lazenby Liberty, was later in 1875 to open the most famous Oriental emporium of all. Sir Rutherford Alcock's *Capital of the Tycoon* (1863) contained some of the earliest illustrations of Japanese prints, and more were shown in J. M. W. Silver's *Sketches of Japanese Manners and Customs* (1867).

One of the earliest interiors to incorporate decoration unequivocally Japanese in inspiration was the Grill Room in the South Kensington Museum, whose stove, designed by Sir E. J. Poynter in 1866, displays many of the motifs which were to become the clichés of the Anglo-Japanese style. In the same year W. E. Nesfield designed a lodge for Kew Gardens which combined red brick and Japanese ornament (badges, or 'pies' as Nesfield called them). In 1867 his favourite cabinet-maker and sculptor, James Forsyth, gave as a wedding present to R. Norman Shaw, the architect, an unequivocally Japanese screen, which may have been designed by Forsyth or Nesfield. By 1866 the Royal Worcester

Porcelain factory was manufacturing Japanese-style ceramics and in the late 1860s Godwin began to design furniture inspired by Japanese models.

Thus from 1862 there was a growing interest in Japanese design and by the end of the decade Anglo-Japanese was an established style, which usually went in tandem with Queen Anne red brick and white paint. One of the later converts was Thomas Jeckyll, who designed furniture and metalwork using Japanese motifs until his madness in 1877.

Moorish and Indian ornament continued at the same time to be employed, particularly in those houses decorated by Owen Jones, whose Alhambra Court at the Crystal Palace, transferred from Hyde Park to Sydenham in 1853, was a show-piece of his favourite style. In 1865 Jones designed the decoration of the Indian and Oriental Courts at the South Kensington Museum, providing another official display of Islamic ornament, while his *Examples of Chinese Ornament* (1867) represents a further facet of his exoticism. By the 1860s imports of furniture, metalwork, and fabrics from India were so widespread that such products were a common element of an English interior. In the late nineteenth century this stream became a flood. English rule over India had the consequence that more and more Indian products came to reflect strong European influence, and bizarre stylistic combinations such as Indian Rococo Revival became commonplace.

It would be misleading to suggest that the exotic was one of the main ingredients of High Victorian design, or that use of exotic styles was widespread. The Anglo-Japanese style of the 1860s rapidly lost any High Victorian characteristics, becoming in the 1870s more superficial, picturesque, and elegant. But any account of design at this period would be incomplete without a representation of the exotic. Exotic ingredients crop up over and over again, even in such apparently unlikely places as William Burges's Cardiff Castle. Owen Jones's demonstration of polychromy of Moorish ornament, and his successful application of its lessons to the decoration of the Crystal Palace, reinforced the High Victorian taste for strong colours. To revert to the culinary metaphor used at the beginning of this introduction, the exotic was a spice which flavoured many things in which its presence might not immediately be suspected.

93
Tea-caddy, japanned papier-mâché, by Jennens & Bettridge, about 1851. This tea-caddy was
presented by the makers to the Museum of Manufactures (now Victoria & Albert Museum) in
1852. Its bright polychrome decoration is in the style of eighteenth-century Chinese 'Canton'
enamels. Jennens & Bettridge of Birmingham were the leading papier-mâché manufacturers
around 1850. Their exhibits at the London 1851 Exhibition were stylistically promiscuous
including naturalistic, Pompeian, Elizabethan, Islamic and Rococo objects.

98

Binding of *Lays of the Holy Land from Ancient and Modern Poets* (1858), royal blue cloth embossed in gold, designed by Albert Warren (1830–1911) and executed by Leighton, Son & Hodge. Warren, son of Henry Warren (1794–1879), a distinguished watercolourist, was a pupil of Owen Jones (1809–74) and assisted him on his *Grammar of Ornament* (1856). *Lays,* a sacred anthology, was illustrated by a distinguished group of artists, including J. E. Millais (1829–96) and Birket Foster (1825–99).

XV

155

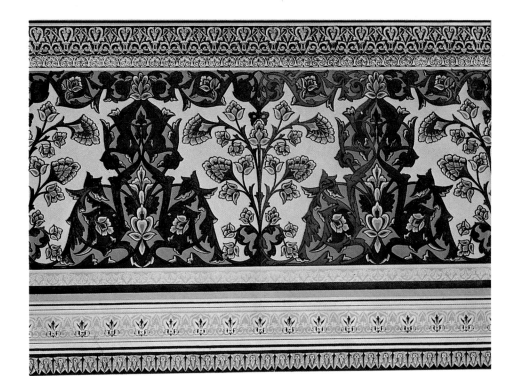

XIV

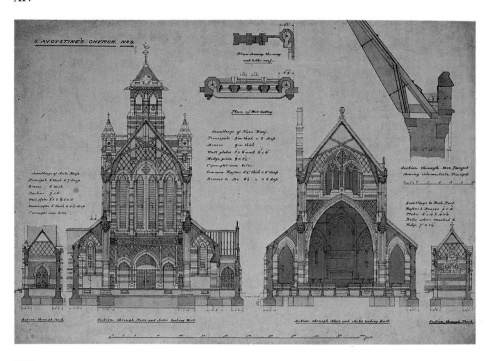

XVI

XV   The Geometric Style
Chalice, silver gilt with champlevé enamel, made by Francis Skidmore & Son of Coventry, about 1851. This chalice, shown at the London 1851 Exhibition, was purchased by the Museum of Manufactures (now Victoria & Albert Museum) for £30 in 1852. It was probably designed by Francis A. Skidmore the younger, who studied historic metalwork and became a member of the Oxford Architectural Society and of the Ecclesiological Society. Skidmore & Son had started to manufacture church plate in 1845.

XIV   The Exotic
Design for a border, gouache, by Owen Jones (1809–74), about 1865. This design, with six others, was purchased by the South Kensington Museum (now Victoria & Albert Museum) for £6 10s at a Sotheby's sale of Jones's effects in 1874. The style of this border is Persian or Indian and corresponds to ceiling designs of similar character and colour in the same group.

XVI   The Geometric Style
Sections and details of St Augustine, Queen's Gate, South Kensington, London, designed by William Butterfield (1814–1900), about 1870. The bold geometry of the whole and the variety of striped and patterned brickwork ornament are typically Butterfieldian. The interior of the church, completed in 1877, was later white-washed but is now returned to its original polychromy, although the 1928 Baroque reredos by Martin Travers remains, in piquant contrast to Butterfield's Gothic.

99

Binding of Edgar Allan Poe, *The Poetical Works* (1858), red morocco embossed in gold, designed
by A. H. Warren (1830–1911). This elaborate edition, more usually bound in cloth, was published
by Sampson, Low, Son & Co.; it includes ornaments designed by W. Harry Rogers (1825–73).
The design was supervised by Henry Cole's friend and publisher, Joseph Cundall (1818–95), who
lectured on bookbinding to the Society of Arts in 1847 and later wrote *Bookbindings Ancient and
Modern* (1881).

100

The Gate of Cairo, called Bab-El-Mutawellee, oil on panel, by David Roberts R.A. (1796–1864), 1843. Roberts travelled in Egypt from 1838 to 1839 and executed numerous drawings of ancient Egyptian and Islamic monuments. Some he worked up into paintings such as this, others were the basis of the monumental lithographs in *Egypt & Nubia* (1846–9), part of a larger work on the Holy Land which brought Roberts international fame.

101
Design for a chair, pen, ink and watercolour, Lucknow, about 1850. The later rulers of Oudh were admirers of European artefacts and encouraged a lasting fashion for furniture which combined Indian ornamental motifs such as antelopes, fishes and tigers, with European forms, in this case a plump Rococo Revival chair, often to comic effect. Such designs are a nice contrast to contemporary European adaptations of Indian ornament.

DESIGN FOR THE DECORATION OF THE ORIENTAL COURT, SOUTH KENSINGTON MUSEUM.
BY THE LATE OWEN JONES.

102
Design for the arcade of the Oriental Court, South Kensington Museum, by Owen Jones
(1809–74), about 1864. Jones was commissioned to design the decorations of the Oriental Court
in 1863. They were executed in about 1864 by Thomas Kershaw, the leading grainer, marbler,
and decorative painter of the age, acclaimed at the Paris 1855 and London 1862 Exhibitions. The
design of this arcade is directly derived from the ornament of the Alhambra.

105

Asia, by John Henry Foley R.A. (1818–74), from the Albert Memorial, 1874. According to the Official Handbook (1874), 'the central figure alone is a female. She is seated on an elephant, and the action of removing her veil is an allusion to the important display of the products of Asia which was made at the Great Exhibition of 1851. The prostrate animal is intended to typify the subjection of brute force to human intelligence; and the surrounding figures . . . all point to the principal divisions of Asia and their respective positions in its civilisation and power'.

At
m
tri
tra
ex
at

rea
an
(17
Hi
Gr
me
its
sid
mo
wh
this
dis
Hig
brie
syn
and
con
boo
Cha
ingi

I
draw
teac
cate
the
Tho

106
Detail of St Paul's House, Leeds, designed by Thomas Ambler (1838–1920), 1878. This vast
factory-warehouse with iron gates by Francis Skidmore was built for Sir John Barran, a pioneer
wholesale clothing manufacturer, brick and terracotta its materials, Veneto-Saracenic its style.
Ambler, a prolific architect, designed a cast-iron and glass warehouse in Basinghall Street, Leeds,
in 1873 and also produced Gothic and Renaissance designs.

sculpture, the ellipsis from Greek art and the circle from Roman art. William Dyce, appointed Superintendent of the Government School of Design at Somerset House, London, in 1838, rejected the human figure, much to Haydon's disgust. Dyce's method of design education, set out in his *Drawing Book* (the first part published in 1843), involved the construction of a grammar of ornament on the basis of simple geometrical figures.

Although practical geometry had a chequered history in the Schools of Design, it remained one of the possible bases of art education. From 1847 to 1848 Richard Redgrave taught botanical drawing at the School of Design in London; the illustrations to his *Manual of Design* (1876) show how he advocated the use of geometry in the conventional treatment of nature. Redgrave, as editor of the *Journal of Design* from 1849 to 1851, was in a position to advertise this approach, which was shared with other members of Sir Henry Cole's circle. Matthew Digby Wyatt had declared an interest in the ornamental use of geometry by publishing *Geometrical Mosaics of the Middle Ages* (1848). Owen Jones's *Grammar of Ornament* (1856) not only contained a plate by Christopher Dresser demonstrating 'the geometrical arrangement of flowers', but his eighth basic proposition stated that 'all ornament should be based on geometrical construction'. Even John Bell, the sculptor and designer, who does not seem to have matched precept with example, argued in 1858 that, for sculpture in an architectural setting, 'there seems but a remote chance of a happy result, unless a geometric laying out of contours and masses, and light and shade, has formed the ground work of the design'.

Architectural theorists also displayed an interest in geometry, notably W. P. Griffiths in *The Natural System of Architecture* (1845) and R. W. Billings in a number of books, including *The Infinity of Geometric Design Exemplified* (1849) and *The Power of Form Applied to Geometric Tracery* (1851). F. C. Penrose's *An Investigation of the Principles of Athenian Architecture* (1851) and Pennethorne's later work on the same subject (1878) are instances of Neo-classical usage of geometric analysis. On the other side of the stylistic divide William White, in a paper in *The Ecclesiologist* entitled 'Modern Design' (1853), explained the Gothic system of proportions based on triangulation.

As for Gothic ornament, A. W. N. Pugin's teachings, expressed in *Floriated Ornament* (1849), provide an interesting parallel to those of Redgrave and the Cole circle; leaves or flowers should be 'drawn out or extended, so as to display their geometrical forms on a flat surface'. It is often difficult to elicit from John Ruskin any unequivocal practical teachings on the subjects he discusses, but his taste in ornament is self-evident. Ruskin admired plate tracery of the most uncompromisingly geometric kind; he also recommended abstract lines and zigzag ornament, geometrical colour mosaics, and coloured patterns of brickwork. All these types of ornament were the stock-in-trade of the Reformed Gothicists of the 1850s, and even more obviously of their commercial followers in the 1860s.

Pugin insisted that elevation should reflect plan and function, which led to the visible separation of each functional unit; but his predilection for picturesque asymmetry and detailing tended to blur the intended distinctions. In the 1840s and early 1850s the Ecclesiologists simplified the form of each unit and substituted massiveness for the picturesque; G. Truefitt's *Designs for Country Churches* (1851) exemplifies this taste for large, simple forms with clear contours, reflecting the influence of George Edmund Street and William White. William Butterfield's All Saints', Margaret Street, London, commenced in 1849, was built up of sharply defined geometric elements, their angularity paralleled by geometric patterning in contrasting brickwork; the interior included geometric painted decoration, tile floors and, on the pulpit, elaborate asymmetric marble disks. Butterfield's work in both simple parsonages and elaborate churches continued throughout his long career to make constant use of geometry in both form and decoration. This is most dramatically apparent in his fonts, a series of masterly geometric variations, many on the theme of the octagonal top and square base. From the early 1850s onwards Street tended towards bare, massive geometric simplicity in his smaller churches, such as Howsham, Yorkshire (1861) and, in more complex buildings, towards constructing a simple imposing mass from the lesser elements, a mass whose apparent geometric clarity often conceals subtle devices to prevent any possibility of stridency, as in St Philip and St James, Oxford (1862). Plate tracery, geometric polychromy, and notched and chamfered profiles were typical of Street in about 1860. William Burges always liked bold geometric shapes, blunt, clear outlines, wheel windows, and bare smooth surfaces, which made windows and ornament all the more effective, as in St Michael, Lowfield Heath, Surrey (1867). In the interior of Cardiff Castle (1865–81), Burges even used Moorish geometric vaulting for ceilings, of a type more usually associated with Owen Jones; however, a similar complex geometry is rendered into Gothic terms in his *dome* over the chancel of St Mary's, Studley Royal, Yorkshire (1871–8).

In the 1850s unbroken rectangularity was a notable feature of many of S. S. Teulon's buildings, together with geometric polychromy, notching, sharply sheered-off mouldings, and tracery simplified almost to extinction. But, notably in country houses such as Elvetham Hall, Hampshire (1859–62), Teulon also employed an elaborate, indeed hectic, variety of geometric forms striped with coloured brick and arranged for violent picturesque effect. Teulon did not have any direct disciples, but other architects made a similar use of abrupt geometry, E. Bassett Keeling, for example, in St George's, Campden Hill, London (1865) and in the decorative details of his controversial Strand Music Hall, London (1864). Grand simplicity recurs in Sir George Gilbert Scott's Brill's Baths, Brighton (1866), surmounted by a vast pointed cast-iron dome, its endless 'coffering' decorated geometrically; and in many square but effective warehouses, including G. Somers Clarke's London Printing & Publishing Company, Smithfield (1860) and E. W. Godwin's massive Anderson's Rubber Company, Stokes Croft, Bristol (1862). Architects of the same generation as Godwin, Philip Webb, R. Norman

Shaw, and W. Eden Nesfield, all used sheer surfaces and clear outlines in the 1860s. But pure geometry culminated in James Brooks' magisterial series of London churches, for example St Saviour's, Hoxton (now Shoreditch) London, apart from retardatory works such as Edmund Scott's St Bartholomew's, Brighton (1874), and the later works of established architects. Commercial buildings also continued to be erected in a coarse and quirky geometric Gothic; Ernest Geldart's designs for the Victoria Fruit Market, Manchester (1868) are typical.

From Butterfield's *Instrumenta Ecclesiastica* (1849 and 1854) onwards, fittings in the Gothic style showed a strong tendency towards geometrical simplicity. This is so both of metalwork designed for special purposes by architects, and that produced by commercial firms such as Skidmore & Son and Hart & Son. James Brooks's candlesticks for St Margaret's, Lewisham, London (1875), are perhaps the masterpieces of pure geometric metalwork. The taste for stiff-leaf carving also reflected that for geometry, and J. K. Collings's *Art Foliage* (1865) contains highly geometric designs, to be compared with those by J. P. Seddon for C. J. C. Bailey's Fulham Pottery (about 1875). Tiles from Pugin onwards were a natural outlet for geometric tendencies, and Butterfield, White, and Seddon all designed notable geometric tiles. However, tiles in undecorated geometric shapes were the most common for arrangement in geometric patterns.

Stencilled ornament was also an encouragement to repetitive geometry; even as late as 1882 W. & G. Audsleys' *Polychromatic Decorations as Applied to Buildings in the Mediaeval Styles* contained strong geometric elements. Geometric marble inlay, which had Ruskin's sanction, was used by Butterfield and Street, and the same motifs were transferred to furniture, tentatively at first, but fully developed in R. Norman Shaw's desk of 1860, shown in the Mediaeval Court of the London Exhibition of 1862. Gothic furniture of the 1862 vintage by Burges, Seddon, Morris, and Webb all used blockish geometric shapes and unbroken surfaces. In the mid to late 1860s commercial designers, such as Charles Bevan and B. J. Talbert, made lavish and sometimes superficial use of blockishness, geometric inlay, and notched and chamfered decoration. J. Moyr Smith employed an even more superficial repertoire of stiff-leaf geometry, derived in part from his master, Christopher Dresser, but displaying little of Dresser's refinement.

Christopher Dresser's designs, although the product of scientific botanical researches, and despite Warington Taylor's criticism of his 'painful geometrical harsh forms', are often very similar to commercial geometric Gothic. On the whole geometric tendencies were less common and less apparent in the non-Gothic styles, but Renaissance Revival and Neo-classical furniture was often decorated with geometric lines, repeated geometric inlay, and highly formalized foliage; metalwork and ceramics in these styles were often built up of pure geometric forms. High Victorian geometry can also be discerned in the severe forms used by the arch anti-Goth, Alexander Thomson, in his Caledonia Road Free Church, Glasgow (1856–7) and elsewhere.

At the London Exhibition of 1862 geometry was visible in a wide range of products: in tiles by Mintons, Maw & Company, T. R. Boote, and the Poole Architectural Company, in church metalwork by Hart & Son, Benham & Froud, Keith & Company, and Skidmores (conspicuously in their Hereford Cathedral choir screen, designed by Sir George Gilbert Scott), in jewellery and ormolu by Howell & James and R. A. Green, in floor-cloths by Messrs Nairn of Kirkcaldy and Messrs Hare of Bristol, and also in Kamptulicon, a patent floor covering, in carpets by Templetons of Glasgow, designed by Matthew Digby Wyatt, who also did tiles for Maws, in wallpaper by Scott, Cuthbertson & Company, in the firm of Treloar's Cocoa-nut Fibre Mats, in Messrs Grainger of Worcester's perforated Parian, and in the Milton vase designed by Pierpoint for R. Attenborough of Piccadilly.

It would be futile to pretend that geometry was at any moment the exclusive language of High Victorian design. The historic styles were so various, and so variously treated, that it is impossible to construct a simple model of the High Victorian artistic universe. But geometry, both on surfaces and in basic forms, does seem to be a constantly recurrent feature in the work of most of the best architects and designers, particularly in the late 1850s and early 1860s – in other words, at the apogee of High Victorian design. This recurrence goes beyond coincidence and must reflect the existence of a transcendent taste, a style. The Geometric style did not survive long enough for its formal language to be developed or classified; it only stuttered into being, and has only recently been identified. But the creative use of geometry provided a vehicle for so many of the most distinguished works of the period that the Geometric style may well come to be recognized as one of the great achievements of High Victorian design.

108

Candlestick, one of a pair, wrought iron with glass and stone cabochons, designed by William White (1825–1900) for the chapel of Bishop's Court, near Exeter, about 1863. Bishop's Court, an ancient palace of the Bishop of Exeter, was remodelled by White in 1860 to 1864 for John Garratt (1812–86). Garratt had in 1859 inherited the house from his father, a wealthy tea merchant, who had been Lord Mayor of London in 1824 to 1825.

109

Pen-stand, gilt brass with ruby glass cabochons, designed by Alfred Waterhouse (1830–1905) for his own use, 1876. By 1876 Waterhouse's reputation, founded on the Manchester Assize Courts (1859), was assured; the Natural History Museum, for which he had been appointed architect in 1866, and Manchester Town Hall were under construction. Present even in this pen-stand is his ability, noted in Eastlake's *Gothic Revival* (1872), 'to invest modern structural requirements with an artistic character . . . Mediaeval in motive if not in fact'.

110

Candlestick, inlaid earthenware, by Wedgwoods, about 1865. This candlestick was given by Wedgwoods to the South Kensington Museum (now Victoria & Albert Museum) in 1865. It is an imitation of the rare French inlaid pottery of the sixteenth century, known as Henri II ware, which was a cult allied to that for Palissy from about 1860. A book by Carle Dulange appeared in 1861, several pieces were shown at the South Kensington Museum in 1862, and in 1863 the Arundel Society issued a volume with photographs of twenty examples. Mintons and Worcester also produced imitations.

111

Jardinière, salt-glazed stoneware, designed by John Pollard Seddon (1827–1906) for the Fulham Pottery, 1877. Seddon's design, in the form of a Gothic stiff-leaf capital, is in the Victoria & Albert Museum. C. J. C. Bailey, proprietor of the Fulham Pottery from 1864, decided in about 1872 to emulate Doulton's artistic stoneware, which had been highly successful at the Paris 1867 and London 1871 and 1872 Exhibitions. Seddon seems to have designed for Bailey from about 1875; they may have met while Seddon's Powell Almshouses near Fulham Palace were building in 1869 to 1870.

116
Design of roofing tiles for Maw & Co. of the Benthall Works, Broseley, by Matthew Digby Wyatt (1820–77), collage of cut-out paper tiles, 1861. Wyatt's first book, *The Geometrical Mosaics of the Middle Ages* (1848), was composed at the suggestion of the terracotta manufacturer, John Blashfield. From 1850 Wyatt designed floor tiles for Maw & Co. who in 1862 published *Specimens of Geometrical Mosaic . . . From Patterns Chiefly Designed & Arranged by M. Digby Wyatt*, with a cover designed by Wyatt.

117
Design of roofing tiles for Maw & Co. of the Benthall Works, Broseley, by Matthew Digby Wyatt (1820–77), pencil and watercolour, 1861. Maw & Co. made continual efforts to improve their technical and design standards, and showed their products at many exhibitions. Their designers also included the Gothic architects George Edmund Street (1824-81), George Goldie (1828–87) and John Pollard Seddon (1827–1906).

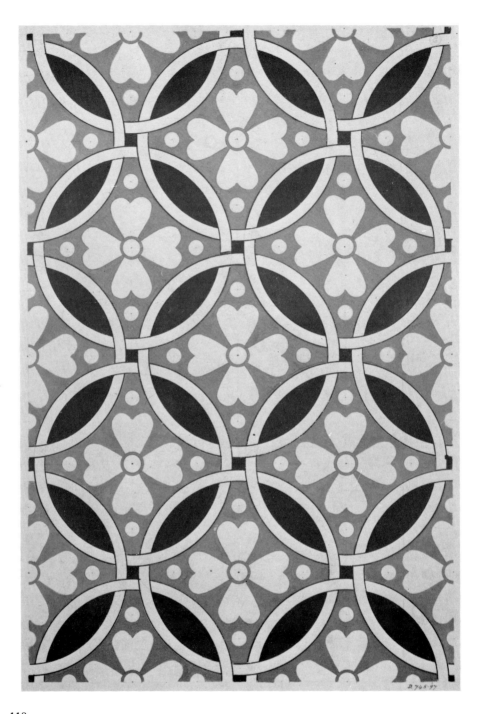

118

Design for flat pattern, gouache, by Owen Jones (1809–74), about 1860. This design, probably for a wallpaper, was made for Jackson & Graham, one of the leading London firms of cabinet-makers and decorators. Many of Jones's wallpaper designs display a similarly direct geometry, influenced by his study of Islamic pattern. As Jones was a successful and prolific commercial designer he is unlikely to have indulged in geometry to this extent without market encouragement.

119

The pulpit of All Saints, Margaret Street, designed by William Butterfield (1814–1900), about 1859. All Saints, commenced in 1849, was the 'Model Church' of the Ecclesiological Society and its first notable display of constructional polychromy; its total cost, including site, was about £70,000. The brilliantly coloured pulpit, incorporating pink granite and red Languedoc, tawny Sienna, green Irish and grey Derbyshire marbles, is a specimen of the 'geometrical colour mosaic' advocated in Ruskin's *The Seven Lamps of Architecture* (1849).

120
The east end of Keble College Chapel, Oxford, designed by William Butterfield (1814–1900), about 1876, after a late-nineteenth-century photograph. Butterfield began work on Keble College in 1867; it was completed in 1883. The Chapel was the gift of William Gibbs (1790–1875), a guano millionaire and deeply committed Christian who added a Gothic chapel by Arthur Blomfield (1829–99) to his own house, Tyntesfield, in 1873 to 1875, while Keble Chapel was being built.

121
Detail of the tower, Humewood Castle, County Wicklow, designed by William White
(1825–1900), 1870. White was commissioned to design Humewood in 1866 by a wealthy
landowner, W. Wentworth Fitzwilliam Hume Dick; escalating costs ended in a protracted law suit
with the builder Albert Kimberly of Banbury, which Dick and White lost in 1876. The material of
the house was granite and its treatment appropriately 'broad, bold and massive', to quote White.

Index

186